CW00432961

the day-by-day method

ASSIMIL®

Writing Japanese with Ease

Kanji stroke-by-stroke

by
Catherine Garnier and Mori Toshiko

adapted for English-speakers
by **Lucas Klein** and **Kiril Savino**

B.P. 25
94431 Chennevières-sur-Marne Cedex
FRANCE

© ASSIMIL 2007   ISBN : 978-2-7005-0355-5

 **Method**

Other Assimil titles available in handy book format with cassettes and CDs

"With Ease" series
Arabic with Ease
Armenian with Ease*
Chinese with Ease vol. 1
Chinese with Ease vol. 2
Writing Chinese with Ease
Dutch with Ease
German with Ease
Hungarian with Ease
Italian with Ease
Japanese with Ease vol. 1
Japanese with Ease vol. 2
Writing Japanese with Ease
New French with Ease
Spanish with Ease

For travelling
Dutch from the Word Go!
French from the Word Go!
German from the Word Go!

Advanced language skills
Using French
Using Spanish

"Business"
Business French

For children
Sing your way to French!

* Available soon

CONTENTS

INTRODUCTION

Since the introduction to Volume 1 (page XI), we've been telling you (honestly) that the most difficult aspect of learning Japanese is the writing. And if you have gotten a little bit lost in the swarm of kanji and kana, then you know what we meant!

But we've also told you that after all, Japanese people know how to read and write, so there's no reason that you shouldn't be able to master the system, as well. The trick is to work at it **regularly**. You're already used to it. And furthermore, just like with hiragana and katakana, there are already many kanji that you have learned to recognize from constant exposure. So you already know the meaning and many of the pronunciations. All that's left is to **put some order into what you know, systematize, fill out the gaps**. That is the first goal of this character volume: it lists, in the order they appear in the 99 chapters of *Japanese with Ease*, the 926 kanji, allowing you to study each one with depth.

But we also want you to go further. And that's the second goal of this book: **you will learn how to learn these and more kanji**, so that you can continue on your own. That's why we have included information along with each kanji character. It may not seem particularly useful at first, but they are in fact precious points to note when you face, on your own, kanji in "real" Japanese texts.

The first step of your study: **read this introduction carefully**, so that you will be able to learn the kanji under the best possible conditions.

1. The kanji: the least you have to know to be able to understand

A brief history

Join us on a voyage through space and time. Imagine, if you will, that you are in first-millennium Japan. You speak Japanese, but you don't have a writing system (this was, of course, the situation for many people around the globe, such as the Anglo-Saxons... one could count the number of written languages of the era on the fingers of one hand, and everyone else "borrowed" from those systems). And then one day you discover, by various methods, how to write! Unfortunately (for us), it is the Chinese system of ideograms. Chinese is a wholly different language from your Japanese, but it's the only way you have of writing. Yet through trial and error, you manage to make it your own.

One day, you decide to take a trip. To keep your family from worrying, you write a note that says, "I'm taking a trip", which is, in Japanese: **tabi ni ikimasu**. But how do you write it, using these infamous ideograms?

A.

You don't worry about what each ideogram means, and use only the sound of each ideogram to convey your message (very approximately, of course, because there are many combinations of sounds in Chinese that do not exist in your language). So you write:

太比仁以幾末寸

太	is pronounced (more or less) **ta** and means *large*
比	is pronounced **hi** and means *to compare*
仁	is pronounced **ni** and means *humane*
以	is pronounced **i** and means *to have*
幾	is pronounced **ki** and means *some*
末	is pronounced **ma** and means *end*
寸	is pronounced **su** and means *inch* (1/30 of a meter)

Each character loses its meaning, or its "**ideo**grammic" quality, and ends up as nothing more than a phonetic. It is exactly this transformation of ideograms that produced the birth of hiragana and katakana.

太	became	太	and then	た	
比	became	比	and then	ひ	
仁	became	仁	and then	に	
以	became	以	and then	い	
幾	became	幾	and then	き	
末	became	末	and then	ま	
寸	became	寸	and then	す	

Of course, this transformation took many hundreds of years, and went through many intermediary steps.

B.

The first system of writing (**A**) must seem a bit long: it takes a long time to write out a complicated ideogram for each syllable. And it's tiring! It seems much easier to retain the ideograms for their meaning. It would be enough to write out the characters for *travel* and *to go*—旅 and 行, respectively. That's much better, isn't it? But then again, you hesitate, because there are two possibilities in front of you:

a) You write the sentence in Japanese, and you use the ideograms for the Japanese word with the same meaning: **tabi** = *travel*, so you write 旅 for the meaning; and **iku** = *to go*, so you write 行 for the meaning. Then you add the particle **ni** and the verb suffixes in hiragana (or, at the beginning, by using the kanji from which the hiragana come from):

旅に(仁)　行き(幾)　ま(末)　す(寸)

b) If you really have to go on this trip in a hurry and you're truly pressed for time, then you take extreme measures: you write directly in Chinese. You don't have to write more than two characters: 旅行, which are pronounced something like they are in Chinese, but adapted to fit the Japanese accent and habit: **RYOKŌ**.

And this is the word that remained in modern Japanese to say *voyage* or *trip*. The word **tabi** is classical Japanese. A great number of words currently in use in Japanese come directly from Chinese. So that's the situation. It isn't simple, and of course it didn't happen all at once, but it's what we've inherited today. Chinese ideograms were in fact poorly adapted to use in Japanese, and it was only after great effort spanning centuries that Japan found a writing system it could call its own, and which would be mostly coherent.

But let's go back to our note saying we've taken a trip.

In **A** case, the kanji give birth to **kana**, the phonetics. In **B** case, we have different pronunciations for each kanji. In possibility **a)**, the kanji are used to write indigenous Japanese words, and we call this kind of writing *kun,* meaning the 'acquired' reading. In kanji dictionaries, the *kun* readings are conventionally noted in hiragana, or, if they're romanized, then in lower-case italics. We follow that usage here. There may be several *kun* readings for any given kanji, as many words can correspond to the same idea, or even the same idea can be expressed as noun, verb, adjective, etc.

In the possibility **b)**, the kanji is used with its (adapted) Chinese pronunciation, and we call this the **ON** (sound) reading. In kanji dictionaries, **ON** readings are noted either in katakana or, if romanized, then in capital letters. This is the method we will be using in this glossary. Again, there may be more than one **ON** reading for any character, as many words imported to Japan from China came at different eras (and as the Chinese pronunciation evolved), or perhaps from different parts of China (and thus from different dialects).

The first question that comes to mind is obvious: how do I know whether the kanji is pronounced in *kun* or in **ON**? There are really very few rules, but nothing is absolute… As long as we're talking about kanji, then we should have an open mind and not strive to find iron-clad rules encased in firm logic!

• A word written with just one character is almost always an indigenous word, and should be pronounced in the *kun* reading. Exceptions are those words or notions that did not exist in native Japanese. For example, as there was no writing system in Japanese, there would obviously not have been a word for *letter*! The kanji 字 *letter* is pronounced in the **ON** reading: **ji** = *letter*.

• **ON** readings are used primarily in compound words. When a word is formed of more than one kanji character (most commonly, two), it is usually read in **ON**. A few compound words do exist in *kun*, but they are relatively rare. Normally, *kun* and **ON** pronunciations are not mixed together in the same compound word, but… there are always exceptions. You will see these exceptions bit by bit during your study, as we have scrupulously respected the conventions of transcription.

The trip is done! Let's hope it helped you in figuring out why the Japanese writing system is as complex as it is today, where Japanese mixes kanji and kana, or why kanji have different pronunciations. But suffice to say that katakana, which have been in existence for a long time (since eighth or ninth century, like hiragana), have only been specifically designated for foreign words other than Chinese since the end of the nineteenth century.

Rules of Writing

Now let's take a look at some of the practical elements of writing kanji. First and foremost, we have the most essential question to answer: "How do you write these characters?" There are so many little lines! But just like kana, there's a **stroke order** to follow, which will not only make the characters easier to remember, but also more aesthetically pleasing, as well. In this volume we have traced out each kanji's order for you line by line. But before we start, you should know a few of the general principles:

—there are two main, incontrovertible principles:

• Kanji characters are written **top to bottom**:

丶 ｔ ｔ 言 言 言 言

一 十 士 吉 吉 吉 声 青 直 喜

• Kanji characters are written **left to right**:

丿 川 川

丿 亻 仁 厃 仔 仔 例 例

—some other useful principles:

• When vertical and horizontal lines cross, write the **horizontal** line first (and remember to respect the earlier two principles):

一 十

一 二 夫 夫

丿 仁 仁 仁 征 征 征 無 無 無

• When a kanji is essentially symmetrical, organized around a central line, write the **central line** first:

丨 小 小
一 十 才 木
ノ ｲ 自 自 自 泊 泊 泊 泊 楽 楽 楽

• Squares are written in **three strokes** (and pay attention to the order of these strokes):

丨 冂 口

• When there are other strokes within a box, the bottom line of the box is the last stroke:

丨 冂 冂 冃 用 国 国 国

Classification system: Radicals

There is often a need to classify kanji: in dictionaries, for sure, but also in an index, telephone books, or file cabinets… Kanji are usually classified by what we call in English **the radical**. The radical is an element (a line or group of lines) common to any number of kanji and which, in most cases, gives some sort of a hint at the meaning of the word.

Example 1

話	語	説	調
to speak	to tell	to explain	to discuss

These kanji all share the speech radical**, the part on the left.** This group of can be its own character, 言, which means "speech". And all kanji that contain this radical have something to do with speech.

Example 2

道	通	送	連	進
way	to pass	to send	to accompany	to advance

These kanji all share the *walking radical*, the lower part. But this element, 辶, does not exist as its own character. Nonetheless, all characters with this radical mean something related to movement.

Example 3

七下三上丈万木世画

All these kanji have the horizontal radical in common. Here, the element can exist as its own character, 一, the kanji for *one*, but it has no meaning as it appears in the above characters.

There are 214 different radicals. You can find a complete table of all Japanese kanji radicals in index 1, from page 211 to 218. You obviously won't need to memorize them all by heart. Simply by studying kanji you will be learning the radicals, and little by little you will find yourself used to all of them. Later on, you will find that knowing the radical is essential to looking up a character in an index or dictionary (cf. introduction to this book's index, p. 257).

2. The kanji in this book: the listing of the kanji

Because you are filled with the great qualities and virtues of curiosity and an enthusiasm to hurl yourself into the kanji right away, admit that you've already looked at the main section of this book: the listing of all the kanji! But let's take a minute or two to understand our method of presentation.

The kanji are laid out, one by one, in the order you encountered them in the 99 lessons of *Japanese with Ease*. On the left of each page, outside the chart, is a small number indicating the lesson concerned.

Let's begin by looking at an example of how each kanji will be presented to you in this book:

中	*naka* (4-4), CHŪ (9-title), -JŪ (30-6): middle, inside 背中 *senaka* (54-13): back 中国 CHŪGOKU (26-title): China 世界中 SEKAIJŪ (76-7): in the whole world
2-3　　　　4	丨　冂　口　中

ON THE LEFT

—**Above**: the kanji

—**Below**: two groups of numbers:

• Two numbers on the left (here, 2-3): 2 represents the number of the radical (cf. appendix 1), while 3 represents the number of strokes in addition to the radical.

• One number on the right (here 4): the total number of strokes in the character.

Complementary information: an asterisk (*) in the lower left section of the grid indicates that the kanji is not part of the 1,945 "common usage" kanji. This kanji, however, is one used in everyday interaction.

ON THE RIGHT

—**Above:**

• First of all, on two or three lines, we have the different pronunciations of the kanji:

  kun pronunciation in lower-case italics

  ON pronunciation in capital letters.

Each pronunciation is followed by numbers in parentheses, which refer to lessons in volumes 1 and 2. Here, for example: *naka* (4-4): the ***kun*** pronunciation *naka* appears for the first time in item 4 of lesson 4. -JŪ (30-6): the **ON** pronunciation JŪ appears for the first time in lesson 30, item 6. The definition of the character then follows.

Complementary information:

• Occasionally different pronunciations will have different meanings. In this case, the meaning is noted after each pronunciation (cf. example p. 22, first kanji).

• Certain **ON** pronunciations will be underlined: this means that they can be used as independent words.

• Certain ***kun*** pronunciations are only used in compound words. In such situations, they will be preceded or followed by a dash, depending on whether they are used in the beginning or at the end of a word (cf. p. 25, 4th kanji).

• An **ON** pronunciation always used at the beginning of compound words will be followed by a dash. Likewise, an **ON** pronunciation always used at the end of in the middle of compound words will be preceded by a dash (cf. p. 33, 1st kanji, p. 30, 5th kanji).

• The other lines in the upper right section are examples of compound words in which the kanji appears. In principle, one example per pronunciation (unless no compound words exist for a given pronunciation, for words rarely used). You will see: the compound word written in Japanese, the pronunciation (in *kun* or **ON** pronunciation), as well as the lesson and item numbers, in parentheses, indicating where the character was first met; finally, we give the meaning of the compound word. Note that sometimes there are no numbers in parentheses. This is when we are showing you a word not given in the 99 lessons. Be sure to take advantage of this "extra word" to increase your vocabulary.

• The asterisk (*) before a compound word suggests that the given pronunciation of the kanji is unique to this particular compound word.

• An (A) sign will indicate what we call an *ateji*, meaning that a combination of characters is being used entirely for its sound, and not its meaning, or that the pronunciation is particular to that combination of characters, and has nothing to do with the pronunciation of either of them separately.

Example: 今朝 is pronounced **kesa** (*this morning*)
Kesa is a simple (non-compound) word, which cannot be separated to know which character corresponds to which part of the word (which we can determine for compound words).

—Below
The kanji is written out line by line so that you can see the appropriate stroke order.

Please note: the kanji presented in this volume appear in their most common form. In this first stage of your study of kanji, we did not want to overwhelm you with a flood of rare pronunciations or usages. You will, in the future, be able to deepen your study with help from more detailed reference and pedagogical works listed in the bibliography.

3. The kanji: how to study them?

Firstly, you have to find your rhythm. You're the one in control. Most important is to keep up the work on a regular basis (that's what keeps the *ease* in *Japanese with Ease*): keep at it **every single day**. Maintain a nice, manageable rhythm like **5 kanji per day**, leaving the 7th day for revision (and so you don't lose your good habits). You can speed up or slow down the rhythm from time to time, but don't cram, and don't lose sight that **the only secret to learning kanji is regular work**.

Secondly, when you first come across a kanji, start by using the information given to you: take a look at the radical (in appendix 1), count the strokes, and go back to the lesson where the character first appeared. This beginning approach is necessary for reminding yourself about the proper context of the kanji.

Finally, just study it: that means...

—train yourself to write the character following the given stroke order: copy it and recopy it until you can write it on your own automatically. Some practical advice: collect your old scrap paper, or... better yet, use a dry-erase board, to keep from amassing pages upon pages of unnecessary paper.

—when you know how to write a character, write it out one more time with its pronunciation—*kun* on the right in hiragana, **ON** on the left in katakana. And pay close attention to the *kun* pronunciations: in verbs and adjectives (and sometimes other words, as well), the final part of the word will be written in hiragana. In the transcription here, we've included it in parentheses.

Example: the transcription will give you:

KEN 見 *mi(ru)*
mi(eru)
mi(seru)
mi(tsukaru)

What you write in your notebook for the kanji should be:

ケン 見 み（る） み（える） み（せる） み（つかる）

And make sure to keep the meaning in mind for each definition.

This will become your mentally embedded image of the kanji! And here again, copy out the character and kana until you can write them automatically.

Then, test yourself: write out several kanji and try to recreate the total image, katakana **ON** and hiragana *kun* pronunciations included. And then try the opposite: write out the words in kana and see if you can fill in the missing kanji.

If you can prepare these quizzes for yourself in advance, say the day before, then it will prove all the more effective.

You must learn how to get used to reading kanji: If you just go over the texts from the lessons in the order they appeared in volumes 1 and 2, that's too easy! With the pronunciation right there beneath the kanji? But we've thought of everything, so we've included everything you need to re-read your lessons without the pronunciation guide (**Appendix 2, pp. 219 to 259) the complete texts from the 99 lessons, as it must be written in 'true' Japanese.**

When you've completed reviewing the kanji from one lesson, you can go to these texts in the appendix and train yourself to read for real. And re-read each lesson as often as possible; that's how you learn to get used to reading kanji "in action". And you'll also be giving yourself another revision, because you'll only be coming across kanji you've already studied.

From time to time in these texts, you can also give yourself little dictation quizzes. That's why we've supplied you with the recordings.

As we've always said, from the beginning: you won't be doing anybody any good by trying to go too fast. Your method should be, and should continue to be: regularity, constant work, and constant revision. If you stay faithful to this method, then you'll astound yourself with your results, week after week after week.

N. B.: *Certain kanji that appeared in the dialogues have not been reprinted here (19 kanji, to be exact). Don't worry, we left them out on purpose. But these kanji are either characters used exclusively in proper names and with special pronunciations, or else very rare characters used quite infrequently. We found it unnecessary to burden your study with these extra kanji.*

15

KANJI

第	DAI (number of each lesson): (number)th
	第二課 DAINIKA (2-number): second lesson
	– 第一次 DAI.ICHIJI (88-ex. 2): first, first time
118-5　　11	ノ ケ ゲ ゲ ゲ ゲ 笋 笃 第 第

一	hito(tsu) (65-1), <u>ICHI</u> (11-2), IK- (1-number), IS- (5-3), IT- (39-7), IP- (37-10): one
	一人 hitori (4-3): one person
	一日 ICHINICHI (39-14): all day long, the whole day
	一ヶ月 IKKAGETSU (34-11): one month
	一緒 ISSHO (5-3): together
	一頭 ITTŌ (39-7): one large animal
	一杯 IPPAI (37-10): a glass/cup of
	(A) 一日 tsuitachi (65-4): the first of the month
1-0　　1	一

課	KA (number of each lesson): section, part
	第一課 DAI.IKKA (1-number): first lesson
149-8　　15	` ゛ 言 言 訂 訶 訶 訶 課 課 課

早	haya(i) (32-9), SŌ: to be early, to be fast
	早く hayaku (1-1): early, fast
	早朝 SŌCHŌ: early morning
72-2　　6	ノ 口 日 日 旦 早

19

1

行	*i(ku)* (1-2): to go, *okona(u)*: to do, to act; KŌ (27-title), GYŌ: to go, to do 通行 TSŪKŌ (82-2): passage, road 行政 GYŌSEI: administration
144-0 6	′ ′ ′ ′ ′ ′ ′ 行 行

暑	*atsu(i)* (1-6), SHO (76-2): to be hot 暑中 SHOCHŪ: heat, in the middle of summer
72-8 12	⟋ 冂 日 早 昇 昇 昇 暑 暑

練	REN (exercise title): to practice, to perfect 練習 RENSHŪ (each lesson, 47-12): exercise
120-8 14	⟍ ⼳ ⼳ 糸 紅 紵 絅 紳 練 練

習	*nara(u)* (64-3), SHŪ (exercise title, 47-12): to study, to review 習性 SHŪSEI: habit, second nature
124-5 11	⼅ ⼅ ⺈ 羽 羽 羽 羽 習 習

言	*i(u)* (37-9: to say, to be called; *koto* (exercise title), GEN, GON (83-5); speech, word 言葉 *kotoba* (all lessons, 38-ex. 1): word, language – 言語 GENGO: language 納言 NAGON (83-5): adviser
149-0 7	′ ⼆ 亠 言 言 言 言

葉	*ha* (22-4), *-ba* (exercise title), YŌ: leaf 葉巻 *hamaki*: cigar 紅葉 KŌYŌ: autumn leaves (red, yellow)
140-9 12	一 艹 艹 艹 芷 莖 莖 葦 葉

入	*hai(ru)* (5-7), **i(ru)* (24-11), NYŪ (23-9): to enter; *i(reru)* (ex. title): to bring in, to put 気に入る KI *ni iru* (24-11): to please 入口 *iriguchi* (79-12): entrance 入院 NYŪIN (23-9): to be in hospital
11-0 2	ノ 入

二	*futa(tsu)* (27-10), *futsu-* (45-5), <u>NI</u> (2-number): the number 2 二人 *futari* (15-4): two people 二日 *futsuka* (45-5): two days, the second of the month 十二月 JŪNIGATSU (74-1): December *二十 *hatachi* (83-4): 20 years old
7-0 2	一 二

展	TEN, -DEN (2-title): exhibition 展覧会 TENRANKAI: an exhibition
44-7 10	７ ７ 尸 尸 屏 屏 屏 展 展 展

見	*mi(ru)* (2-1), KEN (40-title): to look, to see; *mi(eru)* (24-10): to be visible; *mi(seru)* (17-7): to show; *mi(tsukaru)* (92-ex. 4): to be found 見本 *mi*HON (90-ex. 2): sample 見物 KENBUTSU (76-7): visit (monuments…)
147-0 7	丨 冂 冂 月 月 目 目 見

何	*nani* (2-2), *nan* (8-4): what, which? 何時 *nanji* (11-1): what time? 何か *nanika* (34-1): something
9-5 7	ノ イ 亻 仁 仃 佰 何

三	*mit(tsu)* (59-9), *mitsu* (31-2), *mik-* (20-12), <u>SAN</u> (3-number), *SABU (29-9), *SHA (92-9): the number 3 三日 *mikka* (20-12): the third of the month, 3 days 三月 SANGATSU (62-ex. 5): March
1-2 3	一 二 三

朝	*asa* (11-title), CHŌ (3-title): morning; CHŌ (83-7): dynasty 毎朝 MAI*asa* (30-7): each morning (A) 今朝 *kesa* (13-1): this morning 朝食 CHŌSHOKU (3-title): breakfast
74-8 12	一 十 十 古 吉 直 卓 剌 朝 朝

食	*ta(beru)* (3-3), SHOKU (3-title): to eat 食物 *tabemono* (46-13): food 食事 SHOKUJI (26-11): meal
184-0　　9	ノ 入 入 今 今 食 食 食
飲	*no(mu)* (3-5): to drink 飲物 *nomimono*: beverage
184-4　　12	入 今 今 全 食 食 食 飲 飲 飲
卵	*tamago* (3-11): egg
26-5　　7	′ ヒ ヒ 日 卵 卵 卵
四	*yot(tsu)*, *yotsu* (29-9), *yon* (4-title), *yo-* (46-6), *yok-*, <u>SHI</u> (23-7): the number 4 四週間 *yon*SHŪKAN (53-ex. 2): 4 weeks 四時 *yo*JI (46-6): 4:00 四日 *yokka*: the 4th of the month; four days 四月 SHIGATSU (23-7): April
31-2　　5	l 冂 冂 四 四

税	ZEI (4-title): tax, duty 免税 MENZEI: tax-free, duty-free
115-7　　12	一 二 千 千 禾 禾' 利 利 秒 税 税

関	KAN (4-title): barrier, gate 税関 ZEIKAN (4-title): Customs Bureau
169-6　　14	丨 冂 冂 冃 冃 門 門 門 閂 閂 関 関

持	*mo(tsu)* (4-1), JI: to hold, to have 気持 KI*mochi* (48-7): feeling, sensation
64-6　　9	一 十 才 扌 扩 扩 扗 拝 持 持

中	*naka* (4-4), CHŪ (9-title), -JŪ (30-6): middle, inside 背中 *senaka* (54-13): back 中国 CHŪGOKU (26-title): China 世界中 SEKAIJŪ (76-7): in the whole world
2-3　　4	丨 冂 口 中

洋	YŌ (4-6): ocean, Western 太平洋 TAIHEIYŌ: Pacific Ocean
85-6　　9	丶 丶 氵 沪 沪 洴 洋 洋 洋

服	FUKU (4-6): clothing
	洋服 YŌFUKU (4-6): (Western) clothes
74-4 8	丿 刀 月 月 肌 肌 服 服

本	*moto* (16-5), HON (12-10): origin, HON (4-6): book
	本当 HONTŌ (12-10): true, veritable 本屋 HON.*ya* (18-title): bookstore
75-1 5	一 十 才 木 本

酒	*sake* (4-9), SHU: rice wine, alcohol
	酒税 SHUZEI: liquor tax
164-3 10	丶 丶 氵 沪 沪 沂 沔 洒 酒 酒

五	*itsu(tsu)* (59-6), *itsu-*, GO (5-number): the number 5
	五日 *itsuka*: the 5th of the month, 5 days 五月 GOGATSU (23-10): May
7-2 4	一 丆 五 五

買	*ka(u)* (5-4), BAI: to buy
	買物 *kaimono* (5-title): purchases
154-5 12	丶 冂 罒 罒 罒 罒 罒 胃 買 買

物	*mono* (5-title), MOTSU (27-9), BUTSU (30-4), BUSH- (81-8): thing, object 生物 *ikimono*: a living being 書物 SHOMOTSU: book, work of writing 動物 DŌBUTSU (82-9): animal, animate object
93-4　　　8	ノ 一 キ 牛 牛 牜 物 物

緒	SHO (5-3): end, extremity 一緒 ISSHO (5-3): together
120-8　　14	く く 幺 糸 糸′ 結 絈 絈 緒 緒

靴	*kutsu* (5-5): shoe(s) 靴下 *kutsushita* (5-5): sock(s)
177-4　　13	一 廿 甘 苫 苩 革 革 靪 靪 靴

下	*shita* (5-5), KA (31-5), GE (62-1): lower part, bottom; *kuda(saru)* (9-9): to do for me 下着 *shitagi* (80-7): underwear 陛下 HEIKA (68-5): Your Majesty 下宿 GESHUKU (62-1): lodging
1-2　　　3	一 丁 下

着	*tsu(ku)* (5-6), CHAKU: to arrive; *ki(ru)* (54-14): to wear clothes 着物 *kimono* (78-5): a kimono 到着 TŌCHAKU: arrival
123-6　　12	ヽ ヽ ソ ソ 羊 羊 美 着 着 着

26

高	*taka(i)* (5-9), KŌ (32-title): to be high, to be expensive 高速 KŌSOKU (32-title): high speed
189-0 10	﹅ 亠 亠 亠 古 戸 高 高 高 高

六	*mut(tsu)*, *mui-, <u>ROKU</u> (30-7), ROK- (6-number), ROP-: the number 6 六日 *muika*: the 6th of the month, 6 days 六時 ROKUJI (30-7): 6:00 六ヶ月 ROKKAGETSU (80-12): 6 months 六分 ROPPUN: 6 minutes
12-2 4	﹅ 亠 六 六

東	*higashi* (79-11), TŌ (6-title): east 東口 *higashiguchi* (79-11): east entry 東洋 TŌYŌ: the East
75-4 8	一 厂 厂 百 亩 申 東 東

京	*miyako*, KYŌ (6-title): capital 東京 TŌKYŌ (6-title): Tokyo 上京 JŌKYŌ (80-12): to go to the capital
8-6 8	﹅ 亠 宀 占 古 亨 京 京

知	*shi(ru)* (6-1), CHI (67-7), -JI (96-2): to know
	知人 CHIJIN (67-7): friend, acquaintance
111-3　　8	ノ　ヒ　ヒ　午　矢　知　知　知

目	*me* (6-4), MOKU: eye; -*me* (31-8): (number)th
	目的 MOKUTEKI: goal
109-0　　5	l　冂　冂　月　目

黒	*kuro(i)* (96-8), KOKU: to be black
	黒板 KOKUBAN: blackboard
203-0　　11	l　冂　冃　日　甲　甲　里　里　黒　黒

| 駅 | EKI (6-4): train station, bus stop |
| 187-4　　14 | l　厂　厂　兀　丗　馬　馬　馬´　馬′　馬⁷　駅　駅 |

歩	*aru(ku)* (6-4): to walk; HO (82-2), -PO (31-3): step, pace
	歩行者 HOKŌSHA (82-2): pedestrian
	一歩 IPPO (99-12): one step
77-4　　8	l　ト　止　止　牛　歩　歩　歩

近	*chika(i)* (6-5), KIN (47-9): to be close 近く *chikaku* (57-12): proximity 最近 SAIKIN (47-9): recently
162-4　　7	ノ　ｒ　ｆ　斤　斥　近　近

渋	*shibu(i)*, SHŪ, JŪ: to be sober, bare; astringent 渋谷 *shibuya* (6-6): Shibuya 渋滞 JŪTAI: traffic jam, congestion
85-8　　11	丶　丶　氵　汁　汁　浐　渋　渋　渋　渋

谷	*tani, ya* (6-6): valley 谷川 *tanigawa*: mountain stream
150-0　　7	ノ　ハ　グ　父　公　谷　谷

電	DEN (6-6): electricity – electronic 電話 DENWA (13-10): telephone 電子 DENSHI: electron
173-5　　13	一　ニ　戸　币　币　雨　雪　雪　雪　電

車	*kuruma* (34-7), SHA (6-6): vehicle, car 自動車 JIDŌSHA (23-7): car
159-0　　7	一　ｒ　戸　戸　百　亘　車

29

水	*mizu* (31-11), SUI (6-8): water 水色 *mizuiro* (31-11): pale blue 水族館 SUIZOKUKAN (6-8): aquarium
85-0　　　4	丿 刀 水 水

族	ZOKU (6-8): clan, tribe 家族 KAZOKU (67-7): family
70-7　　　11	亠 す 方 方 扩 拧 抟 族 族

館	KAN (6-8): hall, vast residence 大使館 TAISHIKAN (95-1): embassy
184-8　　　16	𠆢 𠆢 全 食 食 食 飠 飣 飣 節 館

店	*mise* (6-10), TEN (12-title): store, shop 店員 TEN.IN: store employee
53-5　　　8	丶 亠 广 广 庁 庐 店 店

七	*nana(tsu)*, *nano-, *nana* (7-number), <u>SHICHI</u> (55-13): the number 7 七日 *nanoka*: 7th of the month, 7 days 七月 SHICHIGATSU (55-13): July
1-1　　　2	一 七

八	*yat(tsu)*, *yatsu* (93-7), **yō-*, <u>HACHI</u> (11-ex. 3), HAK- (8-number), HAS- (69-3), HAT-, HAP-: the number 8
	八日 *yōka*: the 8th of the month, 8 days 第八課 DAIHAKKA (8-number): 8th lesson 八歳 HASSAI (69-3): 8 years old 八分 HAPPUN: 8 minutes

12-0　　　2	ノ　　八

映	*utsu(su)*, EI (8-title): to reflect, to project
	映画 EIGA (8-title): cinema, film, the movies

72-5　　　9	丨　冂　冃　日　旫　旫　旫　映　映

画	KAKU: stroke, GA (8-title): image, drawing, painting
	計画 KEIKAKU: project, plan 画家 GAKA: painter, artist

102-3　　　8	一　丆　丆　帀　雨　面　画　画

昨	SAKU (78-3): past
	昨年 SAKUNEN (78-3): last year (A) 昨日 *kinō* (8-1): yesterday (A) 一昨年 *ototoshi* (89-4): year before last

72-5　　　9	丨　冂　冃　日　旫　旷　昨　昨

日	*hi* (30-9), *-bi* (16-1), NICHI (16-title), NI (18-7), NIK- (27-3), NIT- (30-10): day, sun; *-ka* (20-12), JITSU (45-subheading): day
	月曜日 GETSUYŌ*bi* (26-11): Monday - 半日 HANNICHI (72-10): a halfday - 日本 NIHON (18-7): Japan - 日航 NIKKŌ (27-3): Japan Air Lines - 日中 NITCHŪ (30-10): middle of the day - 二日 *futsuka* (45-5): the 2nd of the month, 2 days - 翌日 YOKUJITSU (45-subheading): the next day - (A) 今日 *kyō* (11-6): today - (A)昨日 *kinō* (8-1): yesterday - (A)明日 *ashita* (27-ex. 5): tomorrow - (A) 一日 *tsuitachi* (65-4): the first of the month
72-0 4	丨 冂 日 日

友	*tomo* (8-2), YŪ (69-8): friend, companion
	友達 *tomodachi* (8-2): friend 友人 YŪJIN (69-8): friend
29-2 4	一 ナ 友 友

達	*-tachi* (39-2), *-dachi* (8-2): "indicator of plurality"; TATSU (61-7), TASH- (90-6): to reach 人達 *hitotachi* (82-5): people 配達 HAITATSU (61-7): home delivery 達者 TASSHA (90-6): expert
162-9 12	一 十 土 圥 圥 查 幸 查 達 達

来	*kuru* (8-2), RAI (23-13): to come
	来週 RAISHŪ (23-13): next week (A)出来る *dekiru* (57-9): to be possible
75-3 7	一 ㄱ 厂 ㅁ 平 来 来

眼	*me* (8-9), GAN: eye 眼鏡 *megane* (8-9): eye glasses
109-6　　11	丨 冂 月 目 目ㄱ 目ㄱ 目ㅋ 眼 眼 眼

鏡	*kagami*, KYŌ: mirror 双眼鏡 SŌGANKYŌ: binoculars
167-11　　19	𠆢 𠂉 牟 余 金 金 釒 鉱 鉖 鏡 鏡 鏡

忘	*wasu(reru)* (8-9): to forget
61-3　　7	' 亠 亡 亡 忘 忘 忘

九	*kokono(tsu)*, *kokono-* (90-13), KU, <u>KYŪ</u> (9-number): the number 9 九日 *kokonoka* (90-13): the 9th of the month, 9 days 九年 KYŪNEN (71-ex. 2): 9 years
5-1　　2	ノ 九

華	KA (9-title): brilliance, shine 中華料理 CHŪKARYŌRI (9-title): Chinese cuisine
140-7　　10	一 十 艹 艹 芢 芢 莒 莒 萱 華

料	RYŌ (9-title): price, material 料金 RYŌKIN (22-4): price, amount
68-6　　10	` ` ` ` ヅ 半 米 米 米 米 料 料
理	RI (9-title): reason, principles 理解 RIKAI (92-ex. 3): comprehension 理由 RIYŪ: reason, cause
96-7　　11	ˉ T F 王 尹 玗 玾 珒 理 理
今	*ima* (12-11): now; KON (9-1): present, current 今晩 KONBAN (9-1): tonight (A) 今日 *kyō* (11-6): today (A)今朝 *kesa* (13-1): this morning (A) 今年 *kotoshi* (23-2) this year
9-2　　4	ノ 人 今 今
晩	<u>BAN</u> (9-1): evening 毎晩 MAIBAN (62-3): every evening
72-8　　12	l 刀 月 日 日' 日' 晗 晚 晚 晚 晚 晚

34

大	*oo(kii)* (20-9), *oo-* (30-3), TAI (44-7), DAI (9-3): to be big 大雨 *ooame* (85-ex. 3): heavy rain 大変 TAIHEN (44-7): extreme(ly) 大学 DAIGAKU (23-2): university (A)大人 *otona* (44-5): adult
37-0　　3	一 ナ 大

好	*suki* (9-3), KŌ (99-15): liked, appreciated 大好き DAI*suki* (9-3): adored, very appreciated
38-3　　6	く 夕 女 女 好 好

私	*watakushi* (9-4), *watashi* (12-6): oneself; SHI (90-2): private 私達 *watashitachi* (39-2): we, us 私立 SHIRITSU (90-2): private
115-2　　7	′ ′′ 千 禾 禾 私 私

肉	NIKU (9-5): flesh, meat 肉体 NIKUTAI: body, flesh, physique
130-0　　6	丨 冂 内 内 肉

魚	*sakana* (9-5), *uo*: fish
195-0 11	ノ ク ク 冇 冇 角 角 鱼 魚 魚 魚

箸	*hashi* (9-7): chopsticks
118-9 15	ノ ⺊ ⺮ ⺮ 竺 竺 笨 竿 箸 箸 箸

十	*tō* (61-3), JŪ (10-title), JUP- (53-9): the number 10
	十日 *tōka* (61-3): the 10th of the month, 10 days
	十一月 JŪICHIGATSU (67-11): November
	十分 JUPPUN (or JIPPUN) (72-6): 10 minutes
24-0 2	一 十

相	*ai*: reciprocal, SŌ: aspect, reciprocal
	相手 *aite*: partner
	相談 SŌDAN: conversation
	*相撲 *sumō* (10-1): sumo wrestling
109-4 9	一 十 才 才 木 札 相 相 相 相

撲	BOKU: to fight
	* 相撲 *sumō* (10-1)
64-12 15	一 十 才 扌 扩 扩 挫 挫 撲 撲 撲

時	*toki* (10-6): moment, time; JI (11-1): time, hour 時間 JIKAN (13-1): time, one hour 九時 KUJI: 9:00
72-6 　　　10	丨 冂 月 日 日⁻ 日⁺ 旪 旹 時 時

起	*o(kiru)* (11-1): to rise, to wake; *o(koru)* (43-6): to take place; *o(kosu)* (72-10): to raise 起き上がる *okiagaru* (72-10): to get back up
156-3 　　　10	一 十 土 キ 丰 走 走 起 起 起

遅	*oso(i)* (11-3): to be late; *oku(reru)* (51-ex. 1): to be late 遅く *osoku* (33-ex. 1): late
162-9 　　　12	フ コ 尸 尸 屋 屖 屖 遅 遅

夜	*yoru* (11-4), *yo* (11-5), YA (75-13): night 夜中 *yonaka* (11-5): in the middle of the night 今夜 KON.YA (75-13): tonight
36-5 　　　8	亠 广 广 疒 夜 夜 夜

寝	*ne(ru)* (11-4), SHIN (66-10): to sleep; *ne(kasu)* (75-6): to put to sleep 寝室 SHINSHITSU (66-10): bedroom
40-10 　　　13	宀 宀 宀 宀 宇 寍 寍 寢 寝

午	GO (11-8): noon (between 11 AM and 1 PM) 午後 GOGO (11-8): afternoon
24-2　　　4	ノ ⺊ 仁 午

後	*ushi(ro)* (50-ex. 1): behind; *ato* (45-5), *nochi* (69-11): after; GO (11-8): behind, after 食後 SHOKUGO (41-12): after the meal 最後 SAIGO (43-11): last
60-6　　　9	ノ ⺈ 彳 彳 彳 衫 祷 後 後

働	*hatara(ku)* (11-8), DŌ: to work, to perform a job
9-11　　　13	ノ 亻 亻 仁 仨 信 俥 俥 俥 働 働

変	*ka(waru)* (41-title): change, transform; *ka(eru)*: to change, revise; HEN (11-10): transform 変化 HENKA: change, transformation
34-6　　　9	⼂ 亠 亣 方 亦 亦 変 変 変

喫	KITSU, KIS- (12-title): to swallow 喫茶店 KISSATEN (12-title): café, teashop
30-9　　　12	丨 ⼝ ⼝ ⼝ 叶 哇 唓 唓 嘊 喫 喫

茶	SA (12-title), <u>CHA</u> (17-1): tea 茶色 CHA.*iro* (96-8): maroon, the color of tea
140-6　　9	一 十 艹 艹 芝 苂 苤 苳 茶 茶
山	*yama* (12-5), SAN (67-title); -ZAN: mountain 山道 *yamamichi* (72-ex. 4): mountain road 火山 KAZAN: volcano
46-0　　3	丨 山 山
田	*ta* (16-5), -*da* (12-5), DEN: rice field
102-0　　5	丨 冂 冊 用 田
菓	KA (12-8): snacks, cake お菓子 *o*KASHI (12-8): snacks, cake
140-8　11	一 艹 芦 芦 苩 萓 草 菓 菓
子	*ko* (15-1), SHI (12-8): child 女の子 *onna no ko* (15-5): little girl 利子 RISHI (45-7): capital interest * 椅子 ISU (60-11): chair
39-0　　3	フ 了 子

39

12

当	*ata(ru)* (75-11), TŌ (12-10): to correspond to 見当る *mi.ataru* (75-11): to be findable 当然 TŌZEN: necessarily, obviously
42-3　　6	丨丶丷丷当当

13

約	YAKU (13-title): promise 予約 YOYAKU (44-2): reservation
120-3　　9	乚乡幺幺糸糸糸糸約約

束	SOKU (13-title): beam, ream of paper 約束 YAKUSOKU (13-title): promise, appointment
75-3　　7	一厂闩写束束束

人	*hito* (19-2), JIN (13-1), NIN (47-11): person, human being 人々 *hitobito* (37-7): people 日本人 NIHONJIN (36-1): Japanese person 十二人 JŪ.NI.NIN (47-11): twelve people * 一人 *hitori* (44-3): one person * 二人 *futari* (44-4): two people (A)大人 *otona* (44-5): adult
9-0　　2	丿人

前	*mae* (13-1), ZEN (27-3): before, ahead 名前 *namae* (36-1): name, first name 以前 IZEN (57-11): before, earlier
18-7　　9	丶 丷 丷 亣 亣 亓 前 前 前

間	*aida* (31-10), *ma* (47-11), KAN (13-1), GEN (88-14): interval, space 間違う *machigau* (88-4): to be fake, wrong 民間 MINKAN (92-13): civil, private 人間 NINGEN (88-14): human realm
169-4　　12	丨 冂 冂 冋 冐 門 門 門 閂 間

待	*ma(tsu)* (13-1), TAI (69-5): to wait 接待 SETTAI (69-5): greeting, reception
60-6　　9	丿 彳 彳 彳 行 往 往 待 待

随	ZUI (13-2): as such, according to 随分 ZUIBUN (13-2): very, extremely
170-9　　12	了 刀 阝 阝 阝 阝 陏 陏 随 随

13	分	FUN (24-3), -PUN (52-ex. 3): minute; BUN (13-2), BU (53-11): part, section 五分 GOFUN (24-3): 5 minutes 三分 SANPUN (52-ex. 3): 3 minutes 分解 BUNKAI (59-12): to break up, dismantle 大分 DAIBU (53-11): the largest part, majority
	18-2　　4	ノ 八 分 分
	話	*hana(su)* (33-4), WA (13-10): to speak, to tell; *hanashi* (25-6): story 話しあう *hanashiau* (66-1): discuss 会話 KAIWA (94-title): conversation
	149-6　　13	丶 亠 亖 言 言 訁 訂 訐 話 話 話
15	紹	SHŌ (15-title): to help 紹介状 SHŌKAIJO: letter of introduction
	120-5　　11	乙 幺 幺 幺 糸 糸 紀 紹 紹 紹 紹
	介	KAI (15-title): intermediary 紹介 SHŌKAI (15-title): presentation, introduction
	9-2　　4	ノ 人 介 介

小	*chii(sai)* (27-10), *ko* (15-1), *-go* (72-11), SHŌ (25-title): to be small, little 小包 *kozutsumi*: package 山小屋 *yamagoya* (72-11): chalet, mountain house 小説 SHŌSETSU (25-title): novel, fiction
42-0 3	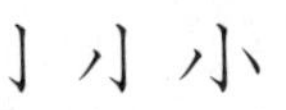
林	*hayashi*, *-bayashi* (15-1), RIN: group of trees, grove
75-4 8	
道	*michi* (15-1), DŌ (32-title): way, road, route 国道 KOKUDŌ (32-3): national highway
162-9 12	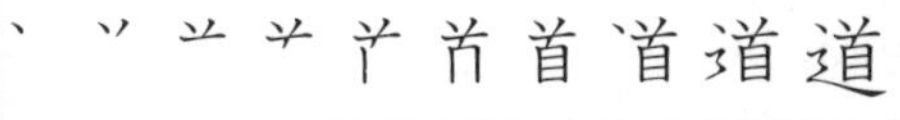
申	*mō(su)* (15-1), to say (high degree) 申し訳 *mōshiwake* (86-14): excuse
102-0 5	
住	*su(mu)* (15-1), JŪ (38-7): to live in 住まい *sumai* (68-7): residence (high degree) 住所 JŪSHO (38-7): address
9-5 7	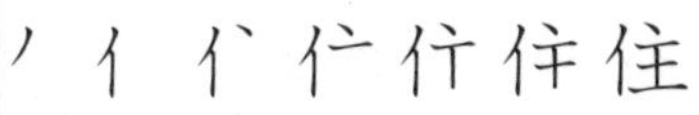

年	*toshi* (23-2), NEN (15-3): year
	毎年 MAI*toshi* (55-3): each year
	来年 RAINEN (26-1): next year
	本年 HONNEN (78-3): this year
51-3　　6	' ⺧ ⻊ ⻏ 仨 年

結	*musu(bu)*, KETSU, KEK- (15-3): to link, knot
	お結び *omusubi* (93-4): rice ball
	結構 KEKKŌ (65-5): perfect
120-6　　12	⼅ ⺐ 幺 乡 糸 糽 紆 結 結 結

婚	KON (15-3): marriage
	結婚 KEKKON (15-3): marriage
38-8　　11	⼥ ⼥ 女 女 妒 妒 娃 婚 婚 婚

供	*tomo*, -*domo* (15-4): companion
	子供 *kodomo* (15-4): child
	お供する *o tomo suru* (26-8): to accompany
9-6　　8	ノ イ 仁 什 件 件 供 供

女	*onna* (15-5), JO (19-5): woman, female
	女の人 *onna no hito* (36-ex. 6): woman
	女優 JOYŪ (18-5): actress
38-0　　3	⼥ 女 女

男	*otoko* (15-5), DAN (62-8): man, male
	男の子　*otoko no ko* (15-5): little boy 美男子　BIDANSHI (94-10): a handsome man
102-2　　7	丨 冂 冂 用 田 旦 男

嬢	JŌ (15-6): lady
	お嬢さん　*oJŌsan* (15-6): lady
38-13　　16	女 女 女 女 娇 娕 嬈 嬈 嬢 嬢

歳	SAI (15-7): age, years old (human)
	二十八歳　NIJŪHASSAI (69-3): 28 years old
77-9　　13	丨 ト ⺊ 此 产 庐 庐 崇 歳 歳

実	<u>JITSU</u> (15-9): reality, *mi*: result, outcome
	現実　GENJITSU (48-11): reality 実は　JITSU *wa* (15-9): in reality, actually
40-5　　8	丶 丷 宀 宀 宔 宔 実 実

再	SAI (15-9), SA (46-6): for the second time, again
	再婚　SAIKON (15-9): remarry, second marriage 再来週　SARAISHŪ (46-6): week after next
13-4　　6	一 厂 冂 丙 再 再

15	
坊	BŌ (15-10): monk お坊ちゃん *o*BOT*chan* (15-10): your young son お坊さん *o*BŌ*san* (85-5): monk
32-4　　　　7	一 十 土 圹 圹 坊 坊
16	
曜	YŌ (16-title): day of the week 水曜日 SUIYŌ*bi* (46-6): Wednesday
72-14　　　18	丨 冂 日 日 日 日 明 明 明 明 曜 曜
天	TEN (16-2): sky, heaven 天気 TENKI (16-2): weather
37-1　　　　4	一 二 チ 天
気	<u>KI</u> (16-2): spirit, feeling, sensation, breath 気分 KIBUN: mood, disposition 電気 DENKI (40-3): electricity
84-2　　　　6	丿 气 气 气 気 気
誘	*saso(u)* (16-5): to invite
149-7　　　14	亠 言 言 言 言 誘 誘 誘 誘 誘

46

考	*kanga(eru)* (16-6), KŌ: to reflect, to think 参考 SANKŌ: reference, consultation
125-0 6	一 十 土 耂 老 考
江	*e* (16-8): bay, cove 江戸(17-10): Edo
85-3 6	丶 丶 氵 汀 汀 江
島	*shima* (16-8): TŌ (67-5): island 半島 HANTŌ (67-5): peninsula
46-7 10	丿 亻 冂 冃 冃 自 鸟 鸟 島 島
寿	*SU (16-10), JU: longevity 寿司 SUSHI (16-10): sushi
41-4 7	一 二 三 夫 丰 寿 寿
司	SHI (16-10): to govern, to administer 司会者 SHIKAISHA: head of meeting
30-2 5	丁 刁 司 司 司

市	*ichi* (17-title): market; <u>SHI</u>: town 市場 *ichiba*: market 市立 SHIRITSU: municipal
50-2　　5	､ 亠 market strokes
箱	*hako* (17-1): box
118-9　　15	ノ ヶ ヶ 竹 竹 竿 筣 箝 箝 箱
右	*migi* (17-1), U: right 右手 *migite*: right hand 右党 UTŌ: the political right wing
30-2　　5	ノ ナ オ 右 右
碗	WAN (17-1): porcelain bowl 茶碗 CHAWAN (17-1): teacup, bowl for tea
112-8*　　13	一 丆 石 石 矿 矿 砀 硫 硫 碗
左	*hidari* (17-3), SA: left 左党 SATŌ: the political left wing
48-2　　5	一 ナ 左 左 左

万	<u>MAN</u> (17-4): 1,0000, ten thousand 五万 GOMAN: 5,0000, fifty thousand
1-2 3	一 万 万

円	<u>EN</u> (17-4); yen (Japanese currency) 十万円 JŪMAN.EN: 10,0000 yen, one hundred thousand yen
13-2 4	丨 冂 冂 円

千	*chi* (68-7), <u>SEN</u> (22-11), -ZEN (17-6): one thousand 二千 NISEN (43-6): two thousand 三千 SANZEN (17-6): three thousand 千代田 *chiyoda* (68-7): Chiyoda
24-1 3	丿 二 千

古	*furu(i)* (17-9), KO (83-2), to be old 古典 KOTEN (83-2): classical literature
30-2 5	一 十 十 古 古

戸	*to* (30-4), -*do* (17-10), KO (95-1): door, house 戸籍 KOSEKI (95-1): registration, register
63-0 4	一 ラ ヨ 戸

代	*kawa(ru)*: to replace; *kawa(ri)* (39-13): replacement; *yo* (68-7), DAI (17-10): generation, period, price 時代 JIDAI (17-10): era, time period
9-3　　　5	ノ　イ　イ　代　代
裏	*ura* (17-13): the back
145-7　　13	亠　亠　亩　审　审　重　重　裏　裏　裏
書	*ka(ku)* (17-13), SHO (38-title): to write, to draw; *-gaki* (22-4): writing 葉書 *hagaki* (22-4): post card 証明書 SHŌMEISHO: certificate, proof
73-6　　10	⁊　⁊　ヨ　ヨ　聿　聿　聿　書　書　書
屋	*ya* (17-ex. 5), OKU (52-5): house, roof, shop タバコ屋 *tabakoya* (20-1): tobacconist 屋上 OKUJŌ (52-5): roof
44-6　　　9	⁊　ヿ　ヷ　尸　屄　屄　居　居　屋

戦	*tataka(u)*, SEN (18-2): to fight 戦後 SENGO: post-war
62-9　　13	丶　丷　丷　当　当　単　単　戦　戦　戦

争	*araso(u)*, SŌ (18-2): to dispute, rival 戦争 SENSŌ (18-2): war
4-5 　　　6	ノ ク ケ 刍 刍 争
平	*hira(tai)*, HEI (18-2): to be flat, to be calm 平仮名 *hiragana* (67-ex. 1): hiragana 平気 HEIKI (62-10): what stays calm, what cannot be disturbed
51-2 　　　5	一 ㇐ 丆 立 平
和	WA (18-2): harmony, peace; Japanese 平和 HEIWA (18-2): peace
30-5 　　　8	ノ 二 千 チ 禾 禾 和 和
家	*ie* (34-1), *uchi* (53-12), *ya* (24-11), KA (18-8), *KE (36-7), *GE (36-7): house, family 家中 *ie*JŪ (59-12): the whole house 家賃 *ya*CHIN (24-11): the rent 家内 KANAI (18-8): my wife
40-7 　　　10	丶 丷 宀 宀 宇 宇 字 家 家 家
内	*uchi* (59-2), NAI (18-8): inside, within 以内 INAI (92-ex. 2): the inside, within the limits of
13-2 　　　4	丨 冂 内 内

留	RU (18-8), RYŪ (78-7): to stay 留守 RUSU (18-8): absence 留学生 RYŪGAKUSEI (78-7): exchange student
102-5 10	留

守	*mamo(ru)* (43-10), SHU, SU (18-8): to protect
40-3 6	守

自	SHI (36-1), JI (18-9): oneself, self 自然 SHIZEN (36-1): nature, natural 自分 JIBUN (18-9): oneself
132-0 6	自

作	*tsuku(ru)* (18-11), SAKU (83-4), SAK- (41-5), -SA: to create, to make, to produce 作品 SAKUHIN (83-4): production, work 作家 SAKKA (83-6): writer 動作 DŌSA: movement, gesture
9-5 7	作

簡	KAN (18-12): brevity, simplicity 簡略 KANRYAKU: simplicity, brevity
118-12 18	簡

単	TAN (18-12): simple 簡単 KANTAN (18-12): simple
47-6　　　9	丶　丷　丷　屵　当　単

毎	MAI (18-14): each, every (+ time notion) 毎度　MAIDO (18-14): each time
80-2　　　6	′　㇉　㇗　勾　勾　毎

度	*tabi* (45-1): time; DO (18-14): time, degree; TAKU (73-3): to compensate for, liberate 度々 *tabitabi* (45-1): often 今度 KONDO (19-ex. 2): this time 支度 SHITAKU (73-3): preparation
53-6　　　9	丶　亠　广　广　庐　庐　庐　庐　度

写	*utsu(su)*, SHA (19-2): to copy 写真　SHASHIN (19-2): photograph
14-3　　　5	′　冖　宁　写　写

真	*ma* (54-5), *man-* (68-11), SHIN (19-2): truth 真中 *mannaka* (68-11): the center, the middle 真理 SHINRI: the truth, a truth
109-5　　10	一　十　广　市　肖　肖　直　真　真

口	*kuchi*, *-guchi* (19-4), KŌ (45-1): mouth, opening, entrance 西口 *nishiguchi* (79-11): west entry 口座 KŌZA (45-1): bank account
30-0　　3	丨 冂 口
文	*fumi* (19-4), BUN (67-8): letter, message, letters, literature 文化 BUNKA (82-1): culture, civilization 文学 BUNGAKU (83-title): literature
67-0　　4	丶 亠 ナ 文
優	YŪ (19-5): excellent, superior 俳優 HAIYŪ (97-11): actor
9-15　　17	亻 亻 俨 俨 俨 傿 傿 優 優 優
歌	*uta* (19-7), KA (19-6): poem, song; *uta(u)* (19-7), KA: to sing 歌手 KASHU (19-6): singer
76-10　　14	一 丁 币 吾 可 哥 哥 哥 歌 歌
手	*te* (31-1), SHU (19-6), *ZU (69-5), hand 手術 SHUJUTSU (53-8): surgical operation, surgery 上手 JŌZU (69-5): skill, expert
64-0　　4	ノ 二 三 手

土	*tsuchi*, DO (19-9), TO: the earth, ground 土地 TOCHI: territory, terrain 土曜日 DOYŌ*bi* (19-9): Saturday
32-0　　　　3	一 十 土

都	TO (58-14): metropolis, capital; *TSU (19-10); moment, circumstances 京都 KYŌTO (60-11): Kyōto 都合 TSUGŌ (19-10): circumstances
163-8　　　11	一 土 尹 尹 者 者 者 者 都 都

合	*a(u)* (71-2), GŌ (19-10): to accord, to combine 場合 *baai* (68-4): case, occasion 連合 RENGŌ (92-ex. 5): league, union, association
30-3　　　　6	ノ 人 ム 今 合 合

次	*tsugi* (19-13), SHI, JI (88-ex. 2): order, next, following 次第 SHIDAI: order, state of things
76-2　　　　6	丶 冫 氵 汐 次 次

機	KI (19-13): occasion; machine 機会 KIKAI (19-13): occasion 飛行機 HIKŌKI (27-2): airplane
75-12　　　16	木 杉 松 栏 栏 棒 機 機 機

会	*a(u)* (27-5), KAI (19-13), *E (99-11): to meet 社会 SHAKAI (88-14): society 会得 ETOKU (99-11): comprehension
9-4　　　6	ノ　入　入　合　会　会

禁	KIN (20-title): forbidden 禁止 KINSHI (82-2): forbidden
113-8　　13	一　十　才　木　林　杕　梺　禁　禁　禁

煙	*kemu(ru)*, EN (20-title): to smoke; *kemuri*: smoke 禁煙 KIN.EN (20-title): no smoking
86-9　　13	丶　ソ　火　灯　炉　炉　炬　煙　煙　煙

辺	*ata(ri)* (32-12), <u>HEN</u> (20-1), -PEN (82-2): surroundings, vicinity 近辺 KINPEN (82-2): surroundings 浜辺 *hamabe*: beach, shore
162-2　　5	フ　刀　刀　辺　辺

遠	*too(i)* (20-3), EN (86-7): to be far, distant 遠く *tooku* (61-ex. 3): far 遠足 ENSOKU (93-title); excursion
162-10　　13	十　土　吉　声　声　袁　袁　袁　遠　遠

隣	*tonari* (20-6): neighbor, neighborhood
170-13 16	阝 阝 阝ー 阝ソ 阝米 阝米 阝米 阝米 阝米 隣

側	*kawa*, *-gawa* (20-9): side 右側 *migigawa* (20-9): right side
9-9 11	丿 亻 亻 仴 伄 伄 俱 俱 俱 側

続	*tsuzu(ku)* (20-12), ZOKU: to follow, continue; *tsuzu(keru)* (99-14): to continue 連続 RENZOKU: continuity, succession
120-7 13	幺 糸 糸 糸 結 結 結 続 続

僕	<u>BOKU</u> (20-13): myself (*male speaker*) 僕達 BOKUTACHI (87-4): us, we
9-12 14	丿 亻 亻 亻″ 亻″ 伴 伴 僕 僕 僕

郵	YŪ (22-title): mail 郵便 YŪBIN (22-4): mail
163-8 11	ノ 二 チ 丢 乒 垂 垂 垂 垂′ 郵 郵

22

便	BEN (24-4): convenience; BIN (22-title): letter, mail 便利 BENRI (24-4): convenient 四百五十三便 *yon* HYAKUGOJŪSANBIN (27-3): flight #453
9-7　　　9	ノ イ 亻 仁 仨 佰 佰 佰 便
局	KYOKU (22-title): bureau 郵便局　YŪBINKYOKU (22-title): post office
44-4　　　7	¬ ¬ ⼫ 尸 月 局 局
航	KŌ (22-4): navigation 航空　KŌKŪ (22-4): aerial navigation
137-4　　10	′ ⼅ 刀 舟 舟 舟 舟′ 舟 舡 舮 航
空	*sora* (48-3), KŪ (22-4): the sky; *muna(shii)* (48-3), *kara(ppo)* (45-9), KŪ: to be empty 空気　KŪKI (75-2): air, atmosphere
116-3　　8	′ ⼍ 宀 宀 穴 空 空 空
金	*kane* (31-14), <u>KIN</u> (22-4), KON: money; metal; KIN, KON: gold 金持　*kanemochi* (87-11): rich 礼金　REIKIN (34-12): fees
167-0　　8	ノ 人 人 今 全 全 金 金

調	*shira(beru)* (22-9), CHŌ: gather information; CHŌ (41-13): harmony
	調子 CHŌSHI (41-13): tone, manner 調査 CHŌSA: investigation
149-8　15	丶 丶 亠 言 言 言 訂 訂 訂 調 調 調

枚	MAI (22-10): *measure word for flat objects*
	三枚 SANMAI (31-3): 3 (as in, three towels)
75-4　8	一 十 才 木 朩 朾 杓 枚

百	<u>HYAKU</u> (22-10), -BYAKU, -PYAKU (95-ex. 2): 100
	五百 GOHYAKU (25-11): 500 三百 SANBYAKU: 300 六百 ROPPYAKU (95-ex. 2): 600
106-1　6	一 ァ ア 百 百 百

仕	*tsuka(eru)* (37-1), SHI (23-title): to serve
	仕事 SHI*goto* (23-title): work, job 仕方 SHI*kata* (44-13): method, way of doing
9-3　5	ノ イ 仁 什 仕

事	*koto* (71-7), -goto (23-title), JI (23-10): fact, event
	記事 KIJI (64-8): newspaper article 用事 YŌJI (86-9): occupation, business
6-7　8	一 ГГ 戸 马 写 写 事

上	*aga(ru)* (72-10): to rise, to get up; *ue* (23-1), JŌ (39-3): upperpart, top 起き上がる *okiagaru* (72-10): to get up 以上 IJŌ (39-3): in addition, above
1-2　　　3	丨 卜 上
息	*iki* (48-5): breathing, *musu (23-1): son 溜息 *tame.iki* (48-5): to sigh 息子 *musuko* (23-1): son
61-6　　10	′ 𠂉 𠂆 白 自 自 自 息 息 息
元	*moto* (40-4), GEN (23-1): base, origin, foundation 足元 *ashimoto* (40-4): footsteps 元気 GENKI (23-1): good health
10-2　　　4	一 二 テ 元
学	GAKU (23-2), GAK- (47-7): to study, to learn, school 学生 GAKUSEI (80-title): student 学校 GAKKŌ (82-1): school
39-5　　　8	丶 ⺍ ⺍ ⺍ 㝳 学 学 学
卒	SOTSU (23-2): soldier, to finish 卒業 SOTSUGYŌ (23-2): graduation, diploma
24-6　　　8	丶 亠 广 产 卆 卒 卒

業	GYŌ (23-2): action, occupation, profession 工業 KŌGYŌ (64-9): industry 農業 NŌGYŌ (64-11): agriculture
75-9　　13	``丶丷丱业业丵芈芈業``

勤	*tsuto(meru)* (23-7), KIN (69-3): to perform a profession 転勤 TENKIN (69-3): mutation, post change
19-10　　12	一 十 卄 芦 芦 苫 革 革 勤 勤

月	*tsuki* (43-7), GETSU (26-11): moon, month; GATSU (23-7): month of a year 十二月 JŪNIGATSU (74-1): December 二ヶ月 NIKAGETSU (34-12): (duration of) two months
74-0　　4	) 冂 月 月

動	*ugo(ku)*, DŌ (23-7): to move 不動産 FUDŌSAN (34-title): real estate agency 運動 UNDŌ (58-7): movement
19-9　　11	一 ニ チ 盲 旨 重 重 動 動

係	KEI (23-7): charge 関係 KANKEI (23-7): link, relation
9-7　　9	ノ 亻 仁 仁 伋 係 係 係 係

社	SHA (23-7): association, company
	会社 KAISHA (23-7): enterprise, company
113-3　　7	` ラ ネ ネ ネ- 社- 社
院	IN (23-9): large building for public use
	病院 BYŌIN (46-subheading): hospital, clinic
170-7　10	˧ ㇈ ㇌ ㇌ ㇌' ㇌' 阝ˊ 阾 陀 阾 院
交	KŌ (23-10): mixture
	交番 KŌBAN (97-1): police station
8-4　　6	' 亠 六 六 亣 交
通	*too(ru)* (57-3), TSŪ (23-10): to pass along; *too(ri)*, *-doo(ri)* (58-8): street; *...(no) too(ri)* (87-12): according to...
	大通 *oodoori* (58-8): avenue, boulevard
	交通 KŌTSŪ (23-10): traffic
162-7　10	㇆ ㇇ マ 丙 甬 甬 甬 `甬 通 通
故	KO (22-10): circumstances
	事故 JIKO (22-10): accident
66-5　　9	一 十 土 古 古 古 古 故 故

毒	DOKU (23-11): poison お気の毒に *o* KI *no* DOKU *ni* (23-11): it's very annoying
80-4　　8	一 十 キ 主 圭 表 青 青 毒

週	SHŪ (23-13): week 一週間 ISSHŪKAN (46-13): one week
162-8　　11	丿 冂 月 冂 用 用 周 周 `周 调 週

退	TAI (23-13): to step back 退職 TAISHOKU (59-12): to retire, retirement
162-6　　9	ㄱ ㅋ ㅋ 艮 艮 艮 `艮 退 退

安	*yasu(i)* (31-9): to be cheap; AN (23-14): to be calm, relaxed 安全 ANZEN (43-10): safety, security
40-3　　6	` ` 宀 灾 安 安

心	*kokoro* (85-2), **goko* (60-11), SHIN (23-14): heart 安心 ANSHIN (23-14): calm spirit
61-0　　4	丿 心 心 心

狭	*sema(i)* (24-2): to be narrow
94-6 9	ノ 犭 犭 犴 犭 狎 狭 狭
利	RI (24-4): benefit, gain 利用 RIYŌ (92-14): use, utilization
18-5 7	ノ 二 千 禾 禾 利 利
音	*oto* (24-6), ON (29-2): noise, sound 足音 *ashioto* (48-2): sound of footsteps 音楽 ONGAKU (47-title): music
180-0 9	` 亠 产 立 立 产 音 音 音
全	*matta(ku)* (48-5), ZEN (24-6): completely, whole 全国 ZENKOKU: the whole country
11-4 6	ノ 入 公 今 全 全
然	ZEN (24-6): to be so 全然 ZENZEN (24-6): (+negation): absolutely not, not at all
86-8 12	ノ ク タ タ タ 夕 夕 殊 殊 然 然 然

聞	*ki(ku)* (29-8), BUN (69-1): to listen, to hear; *kiko(eru)* (24-6): to be audible 新聞 SHINBUN (69-1): the newspaper, daily paper
128-8　　14	丨 冂 冖 冖丶 門 門 門 門 閅 聞 聞
幼	YŌ (24-6): childhood 幼年 YŌNEN: years of youth
52-2　　5	乡 幺 幺 幻 幼
稚	CHI (24-6): young 幼稚 YŌCHI (24-6); child, children
115-8　　13	丿 二 千 禾 禾 禾 秆 秆 秆 稚
園	EN (24-6): garden 動物園 DŌBUTSUEN (39-1): zoo
31-10　　13	冂 门 門 門 周 園 園 園 園 園
階	KAI (24-7): floor, storey 一階 IKKAI: ground level 二階 NIKAI (41-ex. 1): second floor
170-9　　12	乃 阝 阝 阝 阝 阝 阝 阝 阝 階 階 階

眺	*nagame* (24-9): view, panorama
109-6　11	丨 冂 月 目 目 盯 盱 眺 眺

向	*mu(keru)* (75-6), KŌ (75-7): to be turned towards; *mu(kau)* (24-10): to face; *mu(kō)* (39-ex. 5): opposite 方向 HŌKŌ (75-7): direction, orientation
30-3　6	′ ′ 冂 向 向 向

立	*ta(tsu)* (24-10), RITSU (90-1), RIK- (58-8), RIP- (62-4): to stand up; *ta(teru)* (40-13): to stand, to raise 組み立てる *kumitateru* (40-13): to assemble 国立 KOKURITSU (90-1): national
117-0　5	` 亠 产 立 立

賃	CHIN (24-11): rent 賃金 CHINGIN: salary, payment
154-6　13	イ イ 仁 任 任 任 侟 侟 賃 賃 賃

説	SETSU (25-title): opinion, view 説明 SETSUMEI (38-1): explanation
149-7　14	` 亠 言 言 言 言 診 診 診 説

推	SUI (25-3): conjecture, hypothesis 推理 SUIRI (25-3): presumption, guess
64-8 11	一 十 扌 扩 扣 扩 扩 扩 推 推

出	*de(ru)* (27-13), SHUTSU, SHUS- (94-6), SHUT- (89-4), SHUP- (25-4): to go out; *da(su)* (46-9): to bring out 出口 *deguchi* (79-8): exit 思い出す *omoidasu* (89-6): to remember 出席 SHUSSEKI (94-6); present, assistance
17-3 5	丨 屮 屮 出 出

版	HAN, -PAN (25-4): print, printing, edition 出版 SHUPPAN (25-4): edition
91-4 8	丿 丿 丬 片 片 ந版 版 版

主	*nushi* (37-1), SHU (25-7): lord, master; *omo* (40-3): principal 家主 *yanushi*: landlord 主人 SHUJIN (31-10): husband
3-4 5	丶 亠 宁 宇 主

公	KŌ (25-7), *KU (36-7): public 公園 KŌEN (68-12): public park, public garden, plaza 公家 KUGE (36-7): Court nobles
12-2　　4	ノ 八 公 公
思	*omo(u)* (25-11), SHI (50-7): to think 思い違い *omoichigai* (74-title): misunderstood 思想家 SHISŌKA (88-9): thinker
61-5　　9	丿 冂 冊 毌 田 甲 思 思 思
長	*naga(i)* (25-12): to be long
168-0　　8	丨 厂 F 上 長 長 長

国	*kuni* (38-3), KOKU (38-2), -GOKU (26-2), KOK- (69-8): country 国民 KOKUMIN (68-9): the people, nation 天国 TENGOKU (82-2): Heaven 国会 KOKKAI (69-8): the Diet
31-5　　8	丨 冂 冂 冃 用 国 国 国
春	*haru* (26-1): Spring
72-5　　9	一 三 丰 夫 表 春 春 春

語	-gatari (43-6): account; GO (26-2): language
	物語 monogatari (43-6): story, tale 日本語 NIHONGO (47-ex. 4): Japanese language
149-7　　14	亠 言 言 言 言 訂 訂 訢 語 語

悪	waru(i) (26-5), AKU: to be bad, evil
	悪意 AKU.I: ill intentions
61-7　　11	一 丆 广 亖 西 亜 亜 亜 悪 悪 悪

観	KAN (26-7): aspect, view, appearance
	外観 GAIKAN (96-10): outside appearance
147-11　　18	丿 卜 夕 夕 夕 年 年 弁 雀 観 観

光	hika(ru), KŌ (26-7): to sprinkle; hikari (30-5): light
	観光 KANKŌ (26-7): tourism, sightseeing
10-4　　6	丨 丬 丷 业 屰 光

少	suko(shi)(26-8): SHŌ (83-5): a few; sukuna(i): few, small in number
42-1　　4	丿 小 小 少

暇	*hima* (26-9), KA: free time, leisure 休暇 KYŪKA: vacation
72-9　　13	日 日ᐟ 日ᐟ 昭 昭 昭 昭ᐟ 昭 暇

飛	*to(bu)* (39-9), HI (27-title): to fly 飛び立つ *tobitatsu* (43-8): to take off in flight 飛行場 HIKŌJŌ (27-title): airport
183-0　　9	乁 乁 乁 飞 飞 飛 飛 飛 飛
場	*ba* (52-4), JŌ (27-title): place, site 場所 *ba*SHO (52-4): place 練習場 RENSHŪJŌ (52-2): training site, exercise area
32-9　　12	一 十 土 圹 圬 圴 圽 場 場 場
正	*tada(shii)* (99-7), SEI (61-9), SHŌ (44-11): exact, correct, upright 正確 SEIKAKU (61-9): precise 正午 SHŌGO (44-11): 12:00, noon
77-1　　5	一 丁 下 正 正
決	*ki(maru)* (27-2): to be decided of; *ki(meru)* (55-13), KETSU (76-12), KES-: to decide 先決 SENKETSU (76-12): prime urgency 決心 KESSHIN: determination, firm resolve
85-4　　7	' ' 氵 氵 汀 沪 決

成	* _na(ru)_: to become 成田 _narita_ (27-3): Narita
62-2　　　6	) 厂 万 成 成 成

港	_minato_ (51-6), KŌ (27-3): port 空港 KŪKŌ (27-3): airport
85-9　　　12	氵 氵 汢 沣 浐 洪 港 港

迎	_muka(eru)_ (27-4), GEI (94-2): to greet, to receive visitors
162-4　　　7	′ ㇉ 卬 卬 卬 迎 迎

崎	_saki_ (39-9), _-zaki_ (27-5): cape (geography)
46-8　　　11	㇑ 屵 山 山 屵 屵 屵 崚 崎 崎 崎

丈	JŌ (27-6): measures, stature 大丈夫 DAIJŌBU (27-6): no problem
1-2　　　3	一 ナ 丈

夫	FU (66-1), -BU (27-6), FŪ: man, husband
	夫婦 FŪFU: married couple, husband and wife
37-1　　4	一 二 丰 夫
必	*kanara(zu)* (27-7), HITSU (34-7): certainly, inevitably
	必要 HITSUYŌ (34-7): necessary
61-1　　5	` ソ 必 必 必
荷	*ni* (27-9): load
	荷物 *ni*MOTSU (27-9): baggage, luggage
140-7　　10	一 十 サ ガ 芢 芢 芢 荷 荷 荷
配	HAI (61-7), -PAI (27-12): to distribute
	心配 SHINPAI (27-12): worry, anguish
164-3　　10	一 丆 兀 丙 西 酉 酉 酉 配 配
兄	*ani* (27-13), *nii* (71-5), *KEI (94-5), KYŌ: elder brother
	お兄さん *oniisan* (71-5): elder brother 兄弟 KYŌDAI: brothers
10-3　　5	ノ 口 口 尸 兄

所	*tokoro* (27-13), *-dokoro* (34-8), SHO (38-7), -JO (82-10): place, location 台所 DAI*dokoro* (34-8): kitchen 所有 SHOYŪ: possession, property 近所 KINJO (82-10): the vicinity	27
63-4 8		
明	*aka(rui)* (94-8), MEI (38-1), MYŌ (53-5): to be clear, to be bright 明治 MEIJI (88-7): Meiji era (1868-1912) 明後日 MYŌGONICHI (53-5): day after tomorrow (A) 明日 *ashita* (27-ex. 5): tomorrow	
72-4 8		
誕	TAN (29-title): to be born 誕生日 TANJŌBI (29-title): birthday	29
149-8 15		
生	*u(mareru)* (38-4): to be born, *i(kiru)*, SEI (33-7), SHŌ (67-12), JŌ (29-title): to live; *i(keru)* (34-6): to arrange flowers 生活 SEIKATSU (71-4): daily life 一生 ISSHŌ (67-12): whole life	
100-0 5		
火	*hi* (85-5), KA (29-1): fire 火事 KAJI (85-7): a fire	
86-0 4		

芝	*shiba* (29-2); lawn 芝居 *shibai* (29-2): theatre
140-3　　6	一 十 十 サ 芝 芝
居	**i(ru)* (29-2), KYO (34-14): to be located, to reside 入居 NYŪKYO (34-13): to move into (a new house)
44-5　　8	一 コ ユ 尸 居 居 居 居
楽	*tano(shii)* (39-14), GAKU (47-title), GAK- (47-4), RAKU (87-6); to be pleasant; *tano(shimu)* (41-10): to enjoy 音楽会 ONGAKKAI (29-2): music concert 気楽 KIRAKU (87-6): pleasant
75-9　　13	亻 冂 白 白 泊 泊 楽 楽 楽 楽
原	*hara* (29-4): plains, steppe; GEN (76-2): origin 原始 GENSHI: atom
27-8　　10	一 厂 厂 厂 厈 厈 盾 盾 原 原 原
教	*oshi(eru)* (29-4), KYŌ (88-11): to teach 教科書 KYŌKASHO: school book, textbook
66-7　　11	一 十 土 考 考 孝 孝 教 教

取	*to(ru)* (29-6): to seize, to take 書き取り *kakitori* (99-15): dictation
29-6 8	一 丁 干 干 耳 耳 取 取
舞	*ma(u)*: to dance; *mai* (53-title), BU (29-9): dance 見舞 *mimai* (53-title): visit to the ill
136-8 15	一 無 無 舞 舞 舞 舞 舞 舞 舞
伎	KI (29-9): technique 歌舞伎 KABUKI (29-9): Kabuki theatre
9-4* 6	ノ イ 仁 仕 伎 伎
郎	RŌ (29-9): man, *end of a man's name*
163-6 9	' ウ ヲ ヨ 皀 良 郎 郎
怪	KAI (29-9): mystery, apparition 怪談 KAIDAN (29-9): ghost story
61-5 8	' 忄 忄 忰 怿 怪 怪 怪

談	DAN (29-9): conversation 会談 KAIDAN: interview, conference
149-8　15	言 言 言 言 言′ 診′ 診 談 談

演	EN (29-11): acting, dramatic representation 演説 ENZETSU: speech
85-11　14	氵 氵 氵 氵 浐 浐 浐 浐 浨 演 演

奏	SŌ (29-11): to play an instrument 演奏 ENSŌ (29-11): musical performance
37-6　9	一 二 三 丰 夫 表 表 奏 奏

切	ki(ru), kip-, (29-12), SAI (81-8), SETSU (97-1): to cut 切符 kipPU (29-12): ticket 一切 ISSAI (81-8): (+ negative): absolutely not 大切 TAISETSU (99-11): important
18-2　4	一 七 切 切

符	FU, -PU (29-12): mark, sign
118-5　11	丿 𠂉 𠂊 竹 竹 符 符 符 符

先	*saki* (86-8), SEN (29-14); what is in front; *ma(zu)* (39-6): first 先生 SENSEI (33-7): teacher, professor 先月 SENGETSU (73-12): last month
10-4　　6	ノ ⺊ ⺧ 生 牛 先

夏	*natsu* (30-title): Summer 夏休み *natsuyasumi* (30-title): Summer vacation
34-7　　10	一 ⼀ ⺊ 万 百 百 頁 頁 夏 夏

休	*yasu(mu)* (58-12), KYŪ: to rest; *yasu(mi)* (30-title): vacation
9-4　　6	ノ イ 仁 什 休

久	*hisa(shii)* (30-1): to be long (time) 久し振り *hisashiburi* (73-8): long time, many days
4-2　　3	ノ ク 久

麦	*mugi* (30-1): grains: wheat, barley, oats 小麦 *komugi* (30-1): wheat
199-0　　7	一 十 キ 圭 丰 麦 麦

色	*iro* (30-1), SHOKU, SHIKI (72-5): color; sort, kind
	金色　KIN*iro* (85-2): golden, color of gold
	色々　*iroiro* (78-3): of all kinds
	特色　TOKUSHOKU: characteristic
	景色　KESHIKI (72-5): scenery, landscape

| 139-0　　6 | ノ　ク　ク　名　名　色 |

焼	*ya(ku)*: to put fire to, burn, grill; *ya(keru)* (30-1): to be burnt
	日焼け　*hiyake* (54-13): sunburn

| 86-8　　12 | ヽ　火　火　炉　炉　焼　焼　焼　焼　焼 |

瀬	*se* (30-4): fast current, stream
	瀬戸内海　*seto*NAIKAI (30-4): The Inland Sea

| 85-16　　19 | 氵　汀　沪　沖　涑　涑　漸　瀬　瀬 |

海	*umi* (30-7), KAI (30-4): sea
	海上　KAIJŌ: on the sea, maritime

| 85-6　　9 | ヽ　ミ　氵　汇　沪　汝　海　海　海 |

西	*nishi* (30-4), SEI (88-10), SAI (32-1): west 西洋 SEIYŌ (88-10): the West, Occident 関西 KANSAI (32-1): Kansai
146-0　　6	一 丆 币 西 西 西

名	*na* (36-1), MEI (30-4): name 片仮名 *katakana* (80-ex. 1): katakana 名物 MEIBUTSU (30-4): well-known product
30-3　　6	ノ ク タ タ 名 名

太	*futo(i)* (71-9), TAI (30-5): to be fat 大西洋 TAISEIYŌ: the Atlantic Ocean
37-1　　4	一 ナ 大 太

陽	YŌ (30-5): positive energy, the sun 太陽 TAIYŌ: the sun
170-9　　12	⁷ ⁷ ⻖ ⻖⁷ 阝⁷ 阳 陽 陽 陽

強	*tsuyo(i)* (30-5), KYŌ (64-1): to be strong, powerful 強化 KYŌKA: strengthening, reinforcement
57-8　　11	⁷ ⁷ 弓 弘 弘 弘 弭 弭 強 強 強

泳	*oyo(gu)* (30-6): to swim
85-5　　8	丶 丶 氵 汀 汀 汇 泳 泳

昼	*hiru* (30-6): day, daytime 昼寝 *hirune* (30-6): nap 昼間 *hiruma*: the daytime
72-5　9	フ ユ コ 尸 尺 尺 尽 昼 昼

半	HAN (30-7): half 半分 HANBUN (61-4): half
24-3　　5	丶 丶 丷 半 半

岸	*kishi*, GAN (30-8): riverbank, coast 海岸 KAIGAN (30-8): coast
46-5　　8	丨 屮 屮 屵 岸 岸 岸 岸

線	<u>SEN</u> (30-9): line 水平線 SUIHEISEN (30-9): horizon (on the sea)
120-9　15	纟 幺 幺 糸 糸 糸 紵 紵 紵 線 線 線

村	*mura* (30-10): village
75-3　　7	一 十 才 木 村 村 村

貝	<u>KAI</u> (30-11): shell 貝類 KAIRUI (30-11): seashells
154-0　　7	｜ 冂 冂 月 目 貝 貝

類	RUI (30-11): sort, kind, species 書類　SHORUI (38-title): papers, documents
181-9　　18	⺍ ꒳ 半 米 米 类 类 類 類 類

釣	*tsu(ru)* (30-12): to fish
167-3　　11	𠆢 ⺈ 乍 乍 金 金 釣 釣 釣

新	*atara(shii)* (50-1), SHIN (30-12): to be new 新年　SHINNEN (78-1): new year 新婚　SHINKON (65-1): recent marriage
69-9　　13	亠 六 立 立 辛 亲 亲 亲 新 新 新

鮮	SEN (30-12): fresh 新鮮 SHINSEN (30-12): fresh (produce, food)
195-6　17	⺈ ⺈ ⺈ ⺈ 魚 魚 魚 魚 鮮 鮮

旅	RYO (31-1): travel 旅行 RYOKŌ (31-1): travel
70-6　10	⸲ 亠 方 方 方 㫃 㫃 斿 旅 旅
提	*sa(geru)* (31-1): to carry by shoulder strap or hand 手提 *tesage* (31-1): towel, wallet, bag…
64-9　12	扌 扌 扚 扨 护 担 捍 捍 揑 提
鞄	*kaban* (31-1): bag, small case 手提鞄 *tesage kaban* (31-1): tote bag
177-5*　14	一 廾 廿 苫 莒 革 革 靪 靪 鞄
香	KŌ (31-1): fragrance 香水 KŌSUI (31-1): perfume
186-0　9	一 二 千 千 禾 禾 禾 香 香

越	*ko(su)* (31-2): to pass, to go over 追い越す *oikosu* (32-6): to pass, to bypass
156-5 12	土 キ キ 走 走 赴 起 越 越 越

散	*chi(ru)* (89-3), SAN (31-3): to spread out 散歩 SANPO (31-3): walk
66-8 12	一 艹 艹 芋 昔 背 背 散 散 散

雨	*ame* (31-5): rain
173-0 8	一 厂 厂 币 币 雨 雨 雨

降	*o(riru)* (51-3): to descend; *fu(ru)* (31-5): to fall (rain, snow…)
170-7 10	⁷ ⁷ 阝 阝 阝 阽 阽 降 降 降

地	CHI (31-5), JI (66-3): ground 地下 CHIKA (79-6): underground 地面 JIMEN: surface of the ground
32-3 6	一 十 土 圵 坩 地

鉄	<u>TETSU</u> (31-5): iron 地下鉄 CHIKATETSU (31-5): Subway, Underground
167-5　　13	〈 亼 仐 牟 余 金 釒 釒 針 鉄 鉄

乗	*no(ru)* (31-5): to get in a vehicle 乗物 *norimono*: vehicle, means of transportation
4-8　　9	一 二 三 千 乒 乖 垂 乗 乗

赤	*aka(i)* (31-7), SEKI (53-3): to be red 日赤 NISSEKI (53-3): Japanese Red Cross
155-0　　7	一 十 土 チ 赤 赤 赤

青	*ao(i)* (31-7), SEI: to be blue or green 青年 SEINEN: youth, young people
174-0　　8	一 十 キ 主 青 青 青 青

横	*yoko* (31-8): side, flank, horizontal 横切る *yokogiru*: to pass, to cross
75-11　　15	十 木 杧 杧 栟 栟 横 横 横

84

白	*shiro(i)* (31-8), HAKU: to be white 白目　*shirome*: white of the eye 白鳥　HAKUCHŌ: swan
106-0　　5	′ ′ 白 白 白

傘	*kasa* (31-9): umbrella, parasol
9-10　　12	ノ 入 人 个 夵 夵 夵 夵 傘

姉	*ane* (31-10), *nee* (90-4), SHI: elder sister 姉さん　*neesan* (90-4): elder sister 姉妹　SHIMAI: sisters
38-5　　8	く 女 女 女′ 女宀 女宀 姉 姉

縁	*fuchi* (31-11): edge, brink; <u>EN</u>: relation, link 縁側　EN*gawa*: large balcony on Japanese houses
120-9　　15	幺 糸 糽 糽 糽 紵 綀 縁 縁 縁

帰	*kae(ru)* (31-12), KI (45-6): return home 帰国　KIKOKU (45-6): return to one's own country
18-8　　10	′ ′ ′¬ ′¬ ′¬ ′¬ ′¬ 帰 帰 帰

31 銀	<u>GIN</u> (31-13): silver 銀行 GINKŌ (31-13): bank
167-6　　14	𠂉 𠂉 牟 余 金 釘 釘 釦 銀 銀
寄	*yo(ru)* (31-13): to be based on
40-8　　11	丶 宀 宀 宀 宁 宏 害 害 害 寄
部	BU (31-14), HE (44-2): section, part 全部 ZENBU (31-14): totally, wholly 部屋 HEYA (44-2): room
163-8　　11	丶 亠 立 立 咅 咅 咅 咅 部
使	*tsuka(u)* (31-14), SHI (45-12): to use 使い方 tsukaikata (72-ex. 3): way to use 使用量 SHIYŌRYŌ (45-12): tax
9-6　　8	丿 亻 仁 仨 伫 伬 伊 使
32 速	*haya(i)* (89-3), SOKU (32-title): to be fast 速達 SOKUTATSU (61-2): express delivery
162-7　　10	一 ㇆ 戸 戸 市 束 束 凍 速 速

路	RO (32-title): road, route 高速道路 KŌSOKUDŌRO (32-title): highway, expressway
157-6　　13	ㅁ ロ ㄓ 무 무 뮤 무 跅 跞 路 路
伯	(A) 伯父 *oji* (32-1), 伯父さん *ojisan* (47-ex. 5): uncle (A) 伯母 *oba*, *oba(san)*: aunt
9-5　　7	ノ イ イ′ イ′ 伯 伯 伯
父	*chichi* (64-11), *tō* (71-4), FU (94-5): father お父さん *otōsan* (71-4): dad 祖父 SOFU (89-8): grandfather, forefathers
88-0　　4	ノ ハ グ 父
貸	*ka(su)* (32-1): to lend 貸金 *kashi*KIN: lend, amount lent
154-5　　12	ノ イ イ 代 代 伐 貸 貸 貸 貸
末	MATSU (32-1): end 週末 SHŪMATSU (32-1): the weekend
75-1　　5	一 二 キ 才 末

同	*ona(ji)* (36-2), DŌ (32-1): identical, the same 同時 DŌJI: same time, simultaneous
30-3　　　6	丨 冂 冂 同
僚	RYŌ (32-1): companion 同僚 DŌRYŌ (32-1): colleague, co-worker
9-12　　　14	亻 仁 伫 伏 伩 侉 倅 僔 僚
発	HATSU, -PATSU (32-1): to emit, to give birth, to depart 出発 SHUPPATSU (32-1): departure 発明 HATSUMEI: invention
105-4　　　9	フ ヲ ヺ 癶 癶 癶 癶 発 発
最	SAI (32-3): most 最大 SAIDAI: maximum, biggest
73-8　　　12	冂 曰 旦 早 昌 昌 昌 最 最
初	*haji(meru)* (39-2), SHO (32-3): to begin; *haji(maru)*, SHO: to begin, to start 初めて *hajimete* (39-2): for the first time 最初 SAISHO (32-3): at first, at the beginning
18-5　　　7	丶 ラ ヺ ネ ネ 初 初

走	*hashi(ru)* (32-3): to run (*animated being*), to run (*vehicle*)
156-0 7	
混	*ko(mu)* (32-3), KON: to be mixed, to be blocked 混雑 KONZATSU: crowd, crush, traffic jam
85-8 11	
制	SEI (32-4): system, organization 制度 SEIDO: organization, institution, system
18-6 8	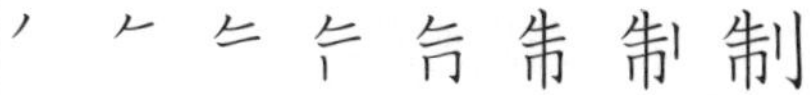
限	*kagi(ru)*, GEN (32-4): to limit 制限 SEIGEN (32-4): restriction, limit
170-6 9	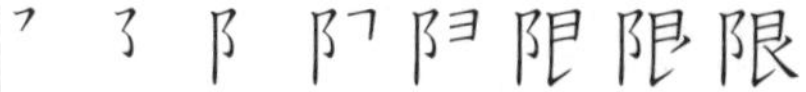
進	*susu(mu)* (32-4), -SHIN (46-14): to advance, to progress 進歩 SHINPO: progress
162-8 11	

追	*o(u)* (32-6): to pursue, to chase
	追い出す *oidasu*: to expel, to chase
162-6 9	´ 亻 ŕ 户 阜 自 ‵自 追
違	*chiga(u)* (74-title), I (32-7): to be different, to vary
	気違い KI*chigai* (82-9): crazy person 相違 SŌ.I: difference
162-10 13	ノ ナ キ 吾 音 查 查 韋 違
反	HAN (32-7): opposition, antagonism
	違反 IHAN (32-7): violation, infraction
29-2 4	一 厂 厅 反
急	*iso(gu)* (32-9), KYŪ (94-11): to hurry
	急に KYŪ *ni* (94-11): quickly, all at once
61-5 9	ノ ク ゎ 乌 刍 刍 急 急 急
汽	KI (32-9): vapor
	汽車 KISHA (32-9): long-distance train
85-4 7	﹑ ﹑ ﹑ ﹑ ﹑ ﹑ 汽

方	*kata* (44-13), *-gata* (33-10), <u>HŌ</u> (32-9), -PŌ (81-8): direction, orientation, method; *kata*: person (high degree) 歩き方 *arukikata*: gait, style of walking 夕方 *yūgata* (33-10): the evening 漢方薬 KANPŌYAKU (81-8): Chinese medicine
70-0　　4	` 亠 方 方
有	YŪ (32-10): to have 有料 YŪRYŌ (32-10): not for free 有名 YŪMEI (37-8): famous
74-2　　6	ノ ナ オ 有 有 有
静	*shizu(ka)* (57-6): calm; *shizu(maru)* (85-2): to calm down 静岡 *shizuoka* (32-12): Shizuoka
174-6　　14	一 十 圭 青 青 静 静 静 静 静
岡	*oka* (32-12): hill
46-5*　　8	丨 冂 冂 冈 冈 岡 岡 岡

捉	*tsuka(maru)* (32-12): to be captured; *tsukama(eru)*: to stop, to capture
64-7* 10	一 寸 扌 扌 护 护 护 捉 捉 捉
罰	<u>BATSU</u>, BAK- (32-12): punishment 罰金 BAKKIN (32-12): penalty, fine
122-9 14	丆 罒 罒 罒 罓 罚 罰 罰 罰
払	*hara(u)* (32-12): to pay
64-2 5	一 寸 扌 払 払
予	YO (32-13): in advance 予算 YOSAN (32-13): budget
6-3 4	乛 マ 予 予
算	SAN (32-13): calculation 算数 SANSŪ (90-8): calculation, arithmetic
118-8 14	ノ トト ケ 竹 竹 竹 算 算 算

足	*ashi* (40-4), SOKU (93-title): foot; *ta(riru)* (32-13), SOKU, -ZOKU: to be sufficient; *ta(su)* (95-3): to add 満足 MANZOKU: satisfactory, sufficient
157-0　　7	丶 丷 ⼝ 口 尸 尺 尸 足
戻	*modo(ru)* (32-13): to retrace one's steps
63-3　　7	一 一 三 ヨ 戸 戸 戻 戻

犬	*inu* (33-1), KEN (37-1): dog 秋田犬 *akita*KEN (37-1): breed of dogs from Akita province
94-0　　4	一 ナ 大 犬
銅	DŌ (33-1): copper 銅像 DŌZŌ (33-1): bronze statue
167-6　　14	ノ 𠂉 ⼂ 牟 余 金 釘 釘 釖 銅
像	ZŌ (33-1): form, portrait 想像 SŌZŌ: imagination
9-12　　14	ノ 亻 伊 伊 伊 伊 伊 像 像 像

感	KAN (33-5): feeling, emotion
	感心 KANSHIN (33-5): admiration
61-9 13	） 厂 厂 后 咸 咸 咸 咸 感 感
野	*no* (33-7), YA (52-9): field, countryside
	野原 *nohara*: the countryside, fields 野球 YAKYŪ (52-9): baseball
166-4 11	冂 日 甲 甲 里 町 野 野 野
英	EI (33-7): England, Great Britain
	英語 EIGO (64-1): English language
140-5 8	一 艹 艹 艻 苎 苎 英 英
飼	*ka(u)* (33-8): to raise an animal
	飼い主 *kainushi* (37-1): an animal's master
184-5 13	𠆢 𠆢 今 今 食 食 飣 飣 飼
夕	*yū* (33-10): evening
	夕べ *yūbe*: evening 夕食 *yū*SHOKU (73-3): dinner, supper
36-0 3	ノ 勹 夕

不	FU (34-title): *negation* 不便 FUBEN (62-2): inconvenient, impractical
1-3　　　　4	一 ア ア オ 不

産	SAN (34-title): *birth, production* 国産 KOKUSAN (96-7): national product
100-6　　11	` 一 亠 立 产 产 产 产 産

捜	*saga(su)* (34-1), SŌ: to search for, to inquire 捜査 SŌSA: research, inquiry
64-7　　10	一 十 扌 扩 押 押 捜 捜

軒	KEN (34-2), -GEN (65-2): *measure word for houses* 一軒家 IKKEN*ya* (34-2): one house
159-3　　10	一 厂 冖 百 亘 車 軒 軒 軒

庭	*niwa* (34-3): garden 庭つき *niwatsuki* (62-ex. 1): with a garden
53-7　　10	` 一 广 庐 庄 庄 庭 庭 庭

別	*waka(reru)* (34-5), BETSU (62-8): to be separate, to be distinct 別々 BETSUBETSU (62-8): separately
18-5　　7	丶 口 口 宁 叧 別 別

妻	*tsuma* (34-6), SAI (66-1): wife …夫妻 FUSA (66-1): Mr. and Mrs…
38-5　　8	一 ラ ヨ ヨ 丰 事 妻 妻

花	*hana* (53-7), *-bana* (34-6), KA: flower 花見 *hanami* (89-title): contemplation of flowers
140-4　　7	一 十 艹 艹 芢 花 花

畳	*tata(mu)* (80-3): to fold, to roll; *tatami* (80-5): tatami mat, straw mat; JŌ (34-8): *measure word for tatami* 八畳 HACHIJŌ (34-6): (room of) 8 tatami
102-7　　12	丶 口 ㎜ 甲 甲 甼 畳 骨 畳

室	SHITSU (34-6): apartment, room 和室 WASHITSU (34-6): Japanese style room 皇室 KŌSHITSU (68-title): imperial family
40-6　　9	丶 冖 宀 宍 宇 宏 宎 室 室

台	TAI, DAI (34-7): support, stage, platform; *measure word for vehicles* 台風 TAIFŪ: typhoon 二台 NIDAI (34-7): two (cars)
30-2 5	㇄ ㄥ 台 台 台
要	YŌ (34-7): essential point 要求 YŌKYŪ: demand, desire
146-3 9	一 ㇒ 冂 両 西 要 要 要
客	<u>KYAKU</u> (34-9): guest, visitor 観光客 KANKŌKYAKU (85-9): tourist, sightseer
40-6 9	' ⼧ ⼧ 宀 灾 灾 宓 客 客
多	*oo(i)* (34-9), TA: to be many, numerous 多分 TABUN: maybe, perhaps
36-3 6	ノ ク タ タ 多 多
敷	*shi(ku)* (89-8): to extend, to spread 敷金 *shiki*KIN (34-12): safety deposit
66-11 15	一 亘 車 重 専 専 尃 敷 敷

34	礼	<u>REI</u> (34-12): politeness, courtesy, ritual 失礼 SHITSUREI (83-13): impoliteness
	113-1　　5	`ラ ネ ネ 礼
36	苗	MYŌ (36-title): young plant, sprout 苗字 MYŌJI (36-title): family name
	140-5*　　8	一 十 艹 艹 苎 苗 苗
	字	<u>JI</u> (36-title): letter, character
	39-3　　6	' 宀 宀 字 字 字
	表	*arawa(su)* (36-1), HYŌ (79-12): to show, to express 代表的 DAIHYŌTEKI (83-8): representative, illustrative, typical
	145-3　　8	一 十 キ 主 丰 声 表 表
	帳	CHŌ (36-3): notebook 電話帳 DENWACHŌ (36-3): phonebook
	50-8　　11	丨 冂 巾 忄 忭 忭 帳 帳 帳 帳 帳

鈴	*suzu* (36-4), RIN: small bell 風鈴 FŪRIN: windchime
167-5 13	ハ ヒ 午 金 金 釒 釒 鈴 鈴

木	*ki* (36-4), MOKU (39-1), BOKU: wood, tree 木曜日 MOKUYŌ*bi* (39-1): Thursday
75-0 4	一 十 才 木

皆	*minna* (36-5), *mina*: all
106-4 9	一 ヒ ヒ 比 比 皆 皆 皆

親	SHIN (36-5): parents, close friends 両親 RYŌSHIN (39-title): both parents
147-9 16	亠 立 立 立 辛 亲 亲 亲 親

戚	SEKI (36-5): relations 親戚 SHINSEKI (36-5): friends, acquaintances
62-7* 11	丿 厂 厂 厂 厈 厈 戌 戚 戚 戚

昔	*mukashi* (36-7): long ago, ancient times
72-4　　8	一 十 艹 艹 芒 昔 昔 昔
武	BU (36-7), MU: concerning the military 武士 BUSHI: warrior
77-4　　8	一 ニ 干 干 武 武 武
段	DAN (36-8): section, degree 段々 DANDAN (36-8): step by step, little by little
79-5　　9	′ 亻 亻 乍 乍 段 段 段 段
民	MIN (36-8): the people 平民 HEIMIN (36-8): the people, common people
83-1　　5	一 ヲ ア 尸 民
舍	(A) 田舍 *inaka* (36-9): the countryside
9-6　　8	ノ 八 合 合 全 全 舍 舍

渡	*wata(ru)* (36-12), TO (88-11): to cross; *wata(su)* (79-8): to give, to stretch 渡来 TORAI: import, come from abroad
85-9　　12	シ　氵　氵　沪　沪　沪　泸　泸　渉　渡

川	*kawa* (36-12): river 川岸 *kawagishi*: riverbank
47-0　　3	ノ　川　川

意	I (36-13): idea, intention 意見 IKEN: advice, suggestion, opinion
61-9　　13	｀　亠　立　立　音　音　音　意　意

味	*aji* (75-11), MI (36-13): taste, flavor; *aji(awu)* (85-9): to taste, to savor 意味 IMI (36-13): meaning, significance, implication
30-5　　8	｜　口　口　叮　吀　吁　味　味

覚	*obo(eru)* (36-14), KAKU (55-11): to remember, to feel, to perceive 感覚 KANKAKU (55-11): feeling, sensory perception
147-5　　12	｀　ｿ　ﾂ　ﾂ　ﾂ　学　労　営　営　覚

37

秋	*aki* (37-11): autumn
115-4 9	ノ 二 千 禾 禾 禾 禾' 秒 秋
亡	*na(kunaru)* (37-2), BŌ: to disappear, to die 亡命 BŌMEI: voluntary exile, emigration
8-1 3	丶 亠 亡
死	*shi(nu)* (37-6), SHI (75-6): to die, <u>SHI</u>: death 死人 SHI.NIN (75-6): the dead, a dead person
78-2 6	一 厂 万 歹 歹' 死
建	*ta(teru)* (37-7), KEN (97-9), *-da(te)* (76-1): construct 建物 *tatemono* (40-6): building, construction 建築 KENCHIKU: architecture
54-6 9	㇇ ⺕ ⺕ 肀 聿 聿 ㇋聿 建 建
杯	HAI, -PAI (37-10): glass, cup, *measure word for full glasses* 二杯 NIHAI: two glasses 一杯 IPPAI (37-10): one full glass
75-4 8	一 十 才 木 木一 杓 杯 杯

籍	SEKI (38-2): register
	国籍 KOKUSEKI (38-2): nationality
118-14　20	⺮ 竺 竿 筦 筰 筩 籍 籍 籍

由	YU (38-5): cause
	…経由 KEIYU (55-5): via…
102-0　5	丨 冂 巾 由 由

美	*utsuku(shii)*, BI (50-title), *MI: to be beautiful
	美しさ *utsukushisa* (85-5): beauty
	美術 BIJUTSU: art, the arts
123-3　9	丶 丷 ⺍ 半 半 羊 羊 美 美

職	SHOKU (38-8): job, work
	職業 SHOKUGYŌ (38-8): profession, career
128-12　18	丆 王 耳 耴 耶 耺 聀 職 職 職

滞	TAI (38-11): to stay
	滞在 TAIZAI (38-11): sojourn, stay (in a country)
85-10　13	丶 氵 氵 泄 泄 泄 滞 滞 滞

38	

在	ZAI (38-11): to exist 存在 SONZAI: existence
32-3　　　6	一 ナ ナ 右 在 在

許	KYO (38-11): to permit, to authorize 免許 MENKYO: authorization, permission 運転免許 UNTENMENKYO: driving permit, license
149-4　　11	` 亠 亖 言 言 訂 訐 訐 許

可	KA (38-11) 許可証 KYOKASHŌ (38-11): permit, authorization
30-2　　　5	一 丁 戸 可 可

証	SHŌ (38-11): proof 証明 SHŌMEI: proof
149-5　　12	` 亠 亖 言 訂 訂 訂 訐 証 証

39

両	RYŌ (39-title): two, couple 両側 RYOgawa: the two sides
1-5　　　6	一 丆 丙 丙 両 両

104

紙	*kami*, *-gami* (39-title), SHI (85-1): paper 手紙 *tegami* (39-title): a letter, a note 表紙 HYŌSHI (85-1): book cover
120-4　　10	く　ㄠ　幺　糸　糸　糸　紅　紙　紙

祖	SO (89-8): ancestor, forefathers (A) お祖父さん *ojiisan* (39-11): grandfather (A) お祖母さん *obaasan* (39-1): grandmother
113-5　　9	`　ラ　ネ　ネ　剂　初　秬　祖　祖

母	*haha* (97-1), *kaa* (71-4), BO (89-11): mother お母さん *okaasan* (71-4): Mom 祖母 SOBO (89-11): grandmother
80-0　　4	乙　口　母　母　母

喜	*yoroko(bu)*: to rejoice; *yoroko(bi)*: joy 大喜び *ooyorokobi* (39-2): great joy
30-9　　12	一　十　吉　声　吉　吉　青　壹　喜

以	I (39-3): by means of 以来 IRAI (59-12): since 以外 IGAI: except, outside
9-3　　5	丶　丷　以　以　以

並	nara(bu) (39-3), HEI: to be aligned, to be in a row 並行 HEIKŌ: parallelism
12-6　　8	丶 丷 丫 丫 汁 汁 並 並

季	KI (39-5): season 四季 SHIKI (66-5): the four seasons
39-5　　8	一 二 千 禾 禾 季 季

節	SETSU (39-5): period, moment; group of words 季節 KISETSU (39-5): a season
118-7　　13	丿 ケ ヶ ヶ 竹 竹 笁 笁 笛 笛 節 節

答	kota(eru) (39-5): to reply; kota(e): response
118-6　　12	丿 ケ ヶ ヶ 竹 竹 竺 竺 竺 答 答 答

首	kubi (39-6): neck, head; SHU (76-7): head, principal element 首輪 kubiwa (82-10): collar 首都 SHUTO (76-7): capital, metropolis
185-0　　9	丶 丷 丷 斗 斗 产 首 首 首

頭	*atama* (50-10), TŌ (39-6): head, *measure word for large animals* 三頭 SANTŌ (39-6): three (large animals)
181-7 16	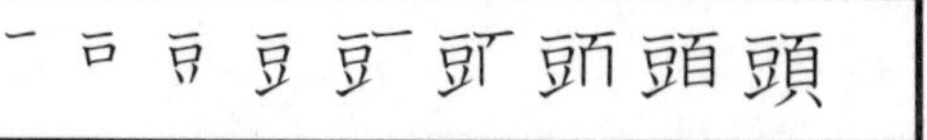
象	ZŌ (39-6): elephant; SHŌ (85-10): image, sign 象牙 ZŌGE: ivory 印象 INSHŌ (85-10): impression
152-5* 12	
耳	*mimi* (39-7): ear
128-0 6	
愛	AI (39-8): love, affection 愛情 AIJŌ: love, tenderness
61-9 13	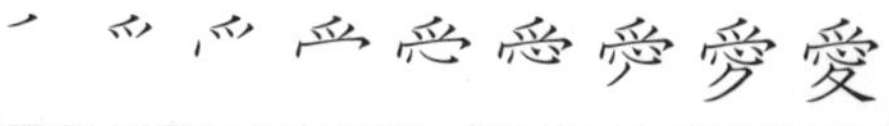
嬌	KYŌ (39-8): attraction 愛嬌 AIKYŌ (39-8): charm
38-12* 15	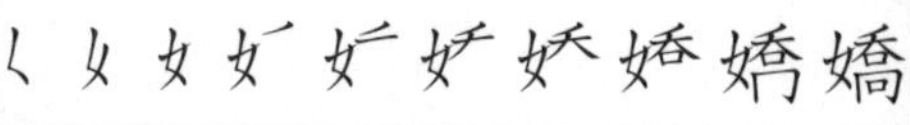

熊	*kuma* (39-8): bear
86-10* 14	⺀ 厶 台 育 能 能 能 熊

似	*ni(ru)* (39-9): to resemble, to look like
	似合う *niau* (71-5): to fit, to suit
9-5 7	ノ イ 亻 化 似 似 似

猿	*saru* (39-9): monkey
94-10 13	ノ 犭 犭 犭 犷 狞 猏 猿 猿

枝	*eda* (39-9): branch
75-4 8	一 十 才 木 杧 材 杖 枝

移	*utsu(ru)* (39-9), I: to move, to transport; *utsu(su)*, I: to transport, to transfer
	飛び移る *tobiutsuru* (39-9): to leap from one place to another
	移動 IDŌ: mobility, transportation, move
115-6 11	ノ 二 千 千 禾 禾 彩 移 移 移

眠	*nemu(ru)* (60-11), MIN (73-9): to sleep; *nemu(i)* (39-10): sleepy
109-5 10	丨 冂 目 目 目' 眅 眠 眠 眠

吠	*ho(eru)* (39-11): to bark
30-4 * 7	丶 冂 口 口 口 吽 吠 吠

妹	*imōto* (39-11), MAI: younger sister 姉妹会社 SHIMAIGAISHA: sister companies
38-5 8	乚 女 女 如 奸 妹 妹 妹

驚	*odoro(ku)* (39-11): to be surprised, stunned
187-12 22	艹 芍 苟 苟' 敬 敬 敬 驚 驚 驚 驚

泣	*na(ku)* (39-11): to sob, to cry
85-5 8	丶 冫 氵 氵' 汁 汁 泣 泣

絵	*e* (39-13), KAI: to draw, to paint 絵葉書 *ehagaki* (39-13): postcard 絵画 KAIGA: painting
120-6　　12	〈 乡 纟 幺 糸 糸 糹 絵 絵 絵

工	KŌ (40-title): worker, work 工場 KŌJŌ or KŌ*ba* (40-title): factory, workshop
48-0　　3	一 丁 工
共	*tomo*, KYŌ (92-4): together, *-domo* (40-2): *indicator of plurality* 私共 *watakushidomo* (40-2): us, we 公共 KŌKYŌ (92-4): common, public
12-4　　6	一 卄 壮 共 共
案	AN (40-2): proposition, idea, plan 案内 ANNAI (40-2): the act of guiding, of giving information, guidance; advertisement
75-6　　10	' 宀 宀 安 安 安 安 案 案 案
製	SEI (40-3): to make, to construct 製品 SEIHIN (40-3): manufactured products
145-8　　14	' 广 乍 告 朱 制 制 製 製 製 製

品	HIN (40-3): things, products 食品 SHOKUHIN (48-12): food products
30-6　　　9	丶 丨 冂 口 吕 品

倉	*kura* (88-7), SŌ (40-5): barn, warehouse, storage house 倉庫 SŌKO (40-5): warehouse, depot
9-8　　　10	ノ 人 人 今 今 今 合 倉 倉

庫	KO (40-5): depot, storage 文庫本 BUNKOBON: pocket edition of a book; paperback
53-7　　　10	丶 亠 广 庐 庐 庐 庐 盾 庫 庫

置	*o(ku)* (40-5), CHI: to place, to put 位置 ICHI: position, location
122-8　　　13	丶 冂 皿 罒 罒 罒 罒 罘 罘 置

務	MU (40-6): to perform a function, to hold a post 事務所 JIMUSHO (40-6): administrative bureau
19-9　　　11	⁊ ⁊ ⁊ 予 矛 矛 矛 敄 敄 務 務

質	SHITSU (40-7): quality 物質 BUSSHITSU (81-8): material
154-8　15	ノ ア ア テ 斤 斉 斉 斉 質 質
問	MON (40-7): to ask 質問 SHITSUMON (40-7): question
30-8　11	丨 冂 冂 冂 門 門 門 問
員	IN (40-9): member of… 議員 GI.IN (69-8): assembly member
30-7　10	丶 冂 口 戶 吊 冒 冒 員 員
失	SHITSU (40-12): error, loss 失業者 SHITSUGYŌSHA (40-12): the unemployed
37-2　5	ノ 二 午 失
者	*mono* (43-9), SHA (40-12): person 悪者 *warumono* (43-9): villain, evil-doer, bad guy 記者 KISHA (69-1): journalist
125-4　8	一 十 土 耂 者 者 者 者

組	*ku(mu)* (40-13): to assemble, to congregate; -*gumi*: group 組合 *kumiai*: association, union 番組 BAN*gumi* (92-4): radio or television program	**40**
120-5　11	く 纟 纟 幺 乡 糸 糸 紅 紅 組 組	

曲	*ma(garu)* (72-9): to turn, to bend; KYOKU (41-5): piece of music 作曲家 SAKKYOKUKA (41-5): composer	**41**
73-2　6	丨 冂 冂 曲 曲 曲	

他	*hoka* (41-9), TA: other 他人 TA.NIN: others
9-3　5	丿 亻 仃 仲 他

断	*kotowa(ru)* (41-9): to refuse; DAN (92-14): decision, break 中断 CHŪDAN (92-14): interruption
69-7　11	丷 丷 半 半 迷 迷 迷 迷 断 断

病	BYŌ (41-12): sickness 病気 BYŌKI (41-12): sickness
104-5　10	丶 亠 广 广 疒 疒 疒 病 病 病

113

41	温	*atata(kai)* (41-13), DO: warm
		温度 ONDO: temperature
	85-9　　12	丶 丶 氵 汀 沪 沪 沪 沪 温 温

43	宇	U (43-4): roof, sky
		宇宙 UCHŪ (43-4): universe
	40-3　　6	丶 宀 宀 宁 宁 宇

	宙	CHŪ (43-4): air, space
		宇宙船 UCHŪSEN: space ship
	40-5　　8	丶 宀 宀 宀 宁 市 宙 宙

	冒	BŌ (43-4): risk, challenge
		冒険 BŌKEN (43-4): risk, adventure
	72-5　　9	丨 冂 冃 冃 冐 冐 冒 冒

	険	KEN (43-4): strategic position
		保険 HOKEN: insurance, guarantee
		保険会社 HOKENGAISHA: insurance agency
	170-8　　11	乛 ß ß 阝 阝 阶 险 险 険 険

球	KYŪ (43-7): sphere, globe 地球 CHIKYŪ (43-7): the planet earth
96-7　11	一 丁 丁 王 王 玎 玗 玗 球 球

点	<u>TEN</u> (43-7): point 出発点 SHUPPATSUTEN (43-7): point of departure
86-5　9	丶 卜 卜 占 占 占 点

星	*hoshi* (43-8), SEI (43-8): star 星座 SEIZA: constellation
72-5　9	丶 冂 冂 日 日 尸 早 星 星 星

惑	WAKU (43-8): to wander 惑星 WAKUSEI (43-8): planet
61-8　12	一 厂 厂 豆 豆 或 或 或 感 惑

果	*ha(te)* (43-9): extremity; KA: fruit, result * 果物 *kudamono* (53-7): fruit
75-4　8	丶 冂 日 旦 甲 甲 男 果

侵	SHIN (43-9): to invade 侵略 SHINRYAKU (43-9): invasion, aggression
9-7　　9	ノ 亻 イ 仒 伊 侵 侵 侵 侵
略	<u>RYAKU</u> (43-9): abbreviation 略語 RYAKUGO: abbreviation, initials
102-6　11	丨 冂 𠃌 田 田′ 田夕 畋 略 略
彼	* 彼方 *kanata* (43-10): over there, far away * 彼女 *kano*JO (71-4): her, she
60-5　　8	′ 彳 彳 彳 犭 犳 彿 彼 彼
敵	<u>TEKI</u> (43-11): enemy 敵国 TEKIKOKU (43-11): enemy country
66-11　15	亠 宀 啇 啇 商 商 商 敵 敵 敵
恋	*ko(u)* (43-11), REN: to fall in love 恋愛 REN.AI: love, passion
61-6　10	` 亠 亠 方 亦 亦 亦 恋 恋

116

容	YŌ (43-13): form, aspect 内容 NAIYŌ (43-13); contents	**43**
40-7　　10	` ' ハ 宀 宀 灾 灾 突 容 容	
興	KYŌ (43-13), KŌ: interest, pleasure 興味 KYŌMI (43-13): interest, pleasure 興行 KŌGYŌ: organization of a show	
134-9　　16	′ イ f 臼 臼 卯 卯 卯 卵 興 興	
離	hana(reru) (44-7): to be far from, to leave	**44**
172-11　　19	亠 玄 卤 离 离 离 离 离 离 離	
座	suwa(ru) (54-12), ZA (45-1): to sit down 座談会 ZADANKAI: round table discussion; group meeting	**45**
53-7　　10	` 亠 广 广 庐 庐 座 座 座	
開	hira(ku) (45-1), KAI: to open; a(ku) (60-8), KAI (89-1): to be open 満開 MANKAI (89-1): full bloom	
169-4　　12	丨 冂 冂 冃 冃 門 門 閂 開 開	

普	FU (45-3): generally
	普通 FUTSŪ (45-3): habitual, usual
72-8 12	`丶 丷 立 芐 苁 竝 竝 並 普 普`

外	*soto* (60-10), GAI (45-3): outside
	外国 GAIKOKU (62-ex. 2): foreign country 外国人 GAIKOKUJIN (45-3): foreigner
36-2 5	`ノ ク タ 列 外`

残	*noko(ru)* (45-6), ZAN (60-8): to stay, subsist
	残業 ZANGYŌ: overtime
78-6 10	`一 歹 万 歹 歹 歼 残 残 残`

| 預 | *azu(karu)* (90-4): to take charge of something, to be entrusted with; *azu(keru)* (45-6): to trust, to leave in care of |
| 181-4 13 | `フ マ 予 予 予 矛 预 预 预 預` |

| 冬 | *fuyu* (45-7): winter |
| 34-2 5 | `ノ ク タ 冬 冬` |

遊	*aso(bu)* (45-7), YŪ: to play, to roam 遊園地 YŪ.ENCHI: amusement park
162-9 12	
増	*fu(eru)* (45-7), ZŌ: to add, to increase 増加 ZŌKA: addition, increase, growth
32-11 14	
翌	YOKU (45-subheading): following (time) 翌朝 YOKUCHŌ: the next morning
124-5 11	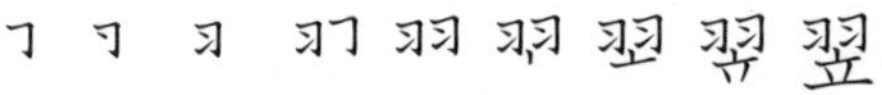
定	TEI (45-9): to specify, to decide 予定 YOTEI (45-9): project, program, prevision 定年 TEINEN (66-6): age limit
40-5 8	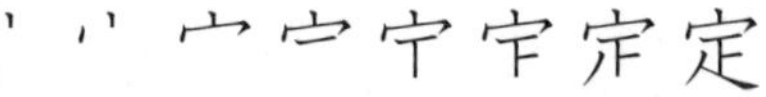
財	SAI (45-9), ZAI: fortune, riches, money 財布 SAIFU (45-9): wallet, purse 財産 ZAISAN: riches, fortune, wealth
154-3 10	

45	
布	FU (45-9), -PU: cloth, to stretch out 分布 BUNPU: distribution
50-2 5	一 ナ オ 右 布
用	<u>YŌ</u> (45-12): employ, use 旅行用 RYOKŌYŌ (65-12): for travel, of travel
101-0 5	) 丿 冂 月 月 用
願	*nega(u)*: to solicit, to request; *negai* (45-13): wish, request
181-10 19	一 厂 厂 盾 盾 原 原 原 願 願
46	
医	I (46-title): medicine 医者 ISHA (46-title): doctor 医学 IGAKU: medicine
23-5 7	一 ア ア ヲ 矢 医
胃	<u>I</u> (46-1): stomach 胃袋 I*bukuro*: stomach
130-5 9	丿 冂 田 田 田 胃 胃 胃

痛	*ita(i)* (46-1): to be in pain, to hurt; *ita(mi)*: pain	
104-7 12	亠 广 广 疒 疒 疒 病 疒 痛	
潰	*tsubu(su)*, KAI (46-2): to crush 潰走 KAISŌ: to make flee, to send into retreat	
85-12* 15	氵 氵 氵 沪 清 清 清 潰 潰	
瘍	YŌ (46-2): ulcer 胃潰瘍 IKAIYŌ (46-2): stomach ulcer	
104-9* 14	亠 广 广 疒 疒 疒 疸 疸 瘍 瘍	
治	CHI (46-4), JI (88-5): to govern, to take care 治療 CHIRYŌ (46-4): care, treatment 政治家 SEIJIKA (88-5): politician	
85-5 8	丶 冫 氵 沪 治 治 治 治	
療	RYŌ (46-4): health 療法 RYŌHŌ: therapy	
104-12 17	亠 广 广 疒 疗 疒 疒 瘆 瘩 瘩 療	

題	<u>DAI</u> (46-4): subject, theme, title 問題 MONDAI (46-4): problem, question
181-9　　18	日　旦　早　早　昇　昰　題　題　題
直	*nao(ru)* (46-4): to be repaired, healed; *nao(su)* (59-2): to repair, to correct, to heal; JIKI (64-6), CHOKU: direct, blunt もう直 *mō*JIKI (64-6): immediately, right away 直接 CHOKUSETSU: direct
109-3　　8	一　十　广　古　肖　直　直
経	*ta(tsu)* (46-8), KEI (55-5): to pass, to go by (time) 経験 KEIKEN: experience
120-5　　11	く　幺　幺　乡　糸　紀　終　経　経　経
舌	*shita* (46-9): tongue
135-0　　6	ノ　二　千　千　舌　舌
押	*o(su)* (46-10): to press, to push
64-5　　8	一　十　扌　扎　扣　拘　押　押

控	*hika(eru)* (46-13): to abstain, to restrain
64-8　　11	一 十 扌 扩 扩' 扩' 扩 挖 挖 挖 控

昇	SHŌ (46-14): to rise 昇進 SHŌSHIN (46-14): advancement, promotion
72-4　　8	丿 口 曰 日 尸 尸 昇 昇

祝	*iwa(u)*: to celebrate; *iwa(i)* (46-14): celebration, festival
113-5　　9	丶 ラ ネ 礻 礻 初 初 初 祝

加	*kuwa(eru)*, KA (47-2): to add 加工 KAKŌ: industrial processing
19-3　　5	フ カ カ 加 加

藤	*fuji* (74-1), TŌ (47-2): wisteria
140-15*　18	艹 艼 芦 菔 萨 莢 莢 藤 藤 藤

特	<u>TOKU</u> (47-3): special 特別 TOKUBETSU (68-2): special, especially
93-6　　10	ノ ニ 十 牛 牛 牜 特 特 特 特

器	KI (47-4): utensil, tool 楽器 GAKKI (47-4): musical instrument
30-12　　15	丶 ロ ロ ロ 叩 叩 罗 哭 罘 器

趣	SHU (47-5): to aim at 趣味 SHUMI (47-5): taste, inclination
156-8　　15	土 走 走 走 赶 起 趄 趣 趣

等	TŌ (47-7): class, degree; equality 高等学校 KŌTŌGAKKŌ (47-7): high school
118-6　　12	ノ ヶ ゲ ゲ 竹 笁 竺 竺 竿 等 等

校	KŌ (47-7): school building 小学校 SHŌGAKKŌ (90-9): primary school, grade school
75-6　　10	一 十 オ 木 杧 杧 柠 柠 校 校

活	KATSU (47-7): life, activity
	活動 KATSUDŌ (47-7): activity, action
85-6　　9	` 丶 氵 氵 汀 汗 汗 活 活

始	*haji(maru)* (92-9), SHI (74-9): to begin; *haji(meru)* (47-7), SHI (74-9): to start something
	年始 NENSHI (74-9): start/beginning of the year
38-5　　8	く 乆 女 奵 妒 始 始 始

| 吹 | *fu(ku)* (47-8): to blow |
| 30-4　　7 | 丶 冂 口 口 叮 吹 吹 |

仲	*naka* (47-11): relation
	仲間 *nakama* (47-11): companion, friend; group, band
9-4　　6	ノ イ 仟 仟 仲 仲

隔	KAKU (47-11): alternate, every other
	隔週 KAKUSHŪ (47-11): every other week
170-10　13	⁊ 彐 阝 阝 阿 阿 隔 隔 隔 隔

集	*atsu(maru)* (47-11), SHŪ: to gather together; *atsu(meru)*, SHŪ: to get together 集団 SHŪDAN: group, organization
172-4 12	ノ イ イ´ イ⺧ 什 佳 隹 隹 隼 集

終	*o(waru)* (48-1), SHŪ: to end, finish 終点 SHŪTEN: last stop (of a bus/train line)
120-5 11	く 乡 纟 纟 糸 糸 紵 紁 終 終

雲	*kumo* (67-6), *-gumo* (48-3): cloud いわし雲 *iwashigumo* (48-3): cirrus clouds
173-4 12	一 厂 广 币 币 雨 雩 雩 雲 雲

浮	*uka(bu)* (48-3): to float
85-7 10	ヽ ヽヽ 氵 氵' 氵ⁿ 浮 浮 浮 浮

世	*yo* (48-3), SE (76-6), SEI (88-5): the world 世話 SEWA (78-3): service, good care 世紀 SEIKI (88-5): century
1-4 5	一 十 卄 世 世

枯	*ka(reru)* (48-4): to wither, to die 枯葉 *kareha* (48-4): dead leaves
75-5　　9	一 十 才 木 朾 朾 杧 枯 枯

落	*o(chiru)* (48-4), RAKU: to fall; *o(tosu)* (73-3): to make fall 落第 RAKUDAI: failure in an exam / a test
140-9　　12	一 艹 莎 莎 莎 莎 茨 落 落

悲	*kana(shii)* (48-4), HI: to be sad 悲劇 HIGEKI: tragedy
61-8　　12	ノ ナ ヲ ヨ 非 非 非 悲 悲

溜	*ta(meru)* (48-5): to accumulate, to collect 溜池 *tame.ike*: reservoir, cistern
85-10*　　13	シ ジ 沙 汐 沔 沔 溜 溜 溜 溜

詩	<u>SHI</u> (48-5): poetry (not Japanese) 漢詩 KANSHI: Chinese poetry
149-6　　13	` 二 言 言 計 計 詰 詰 詩 詩

暮	*kura(su)* (97-7): to live, to spend one's time on sth/doing sth; *ku(reru)*: to finish; *ku(re)*, *-gu(re)* (48-6): end
	日暮れ *higure* (48-6): the end of the day, dusk
72-10　14	一 艹 艻 芦 苜 莫 莫 莫 暮

柿	*kaki* (48-6): kaki tree, persimmon
	柿色 *kaki.iro*: yellow-brown
75-5*　9	一 十 才 木 朾 朾 柿 柿 柿

| 輝 | *kagaya(ku)* (48-6): to shine, to sparkle |
| 159-8　15 | 丿 ⺌ 业 ⺟ 光 灯 炉 焙 焙 輝 |

過	*su(giru)* (48-7), KA: to pass, to surpass; *su(gosu)* (97-7): to spend (one's time on sth); to live
	過去 KAKO: the past
	過程 KATEI: process
162-9　12	丿 冂 冂 冎 咼 咼 咼 渦 渦 過

| 寂 | *sabi(shii)* (48-7): to be sad, solitary, depressed |
| 40-8　11 | 丶 宀 宀 宁 宇 宇 宋 宋 寂 寂 |

命	*inochi* (48-8), MEI (83-2): life, destiny; order, command 人命 JINMEI: human life 命令 MEIREI: order, command
30-5　　8	ノ　ㄥ　ㅅ　合　合　合　命　命

風	*kaze*: wind; FU (62-1), FŪ (48-10): wind, air; appearance, manner (A) 風呂 *furo* (62-1): Japanese bath 日本風 NIHONFŪ (66-4): Japanese-style * 風邪 *kaze* (81-title): a common cold
182-0　　9	ノ　几　几　凡　同　風　風　風

酔	*yo(u)* (48-11): to be drunk 酔っぱらう *yopparau* (48-11); to be drunk
164-4　　11	一　丆　西　西　酉　酉'　酉九　酉比　酔

現	GEN (48-11): current, present 現代 GENDAI (50-1): modern
96-7　　11	一　丁　干　王　玑　玑　珇　珇　珇　現

的	-TEKI (48-11): *suffix for creating adjectives* 現実的 GENJITSUTEKI (48-11): realist
106-3　　8	'　亻　白　白　白　白'　的　的

冷	*tsumeta(i)* (54-7): to be cold, to be frozen; *hi(yasu)* (74-4), REI (48-12): to refrigerate 冷凍 REITŌ (48-12): refrigeration
15-5　　7	` 冫 冫 冫 冷 冷 冷
凍	TŌ (48-12): to freeze 凍結 TŌKETSU: freezing
15-8　　10	冫 冫 冫 凍 凍 凍 凍 凍 凍 凍
売	*u(ru)* (48-12), BAI (48-12): to sell 商売 SHŌBAI (48-12): business, commerce, trade
33-4　　7	一 十 土 声 声 声 売
商	SHŌ (48-12): commerce, trade 商社マン SHŌSHA*man* (97-11): business man, salesman
30-8　　11	` 亠 立 产 产 产 商 商

術	JUTSU (50-title): art, technique 美術館 BIJUTSUKAN (50-title): art museum
144-5　　11	ク 彳 彳 行 休 休 術 術 術

緑	*midori* (50-6): green, greenness
	緑色 *midori-iro* (50-6): green, the green color
120-8 　14	く 幺 糸 糸 糸 糸 糸 糸 緑

非	HI (50-7): wrong, false, *negative prefix*
	非常 HIJŌ (50-7): extraordinary, uncommon
175-0 　8	) ） ナ 才 月 非 非

常	*tsune*, JŌ (50-7): habitual, normal, common
	日常 NICHIJŌ (94-title): daily, ordinary
50-8 　11	' ⌒ ⌒ ⌒ 学 常 常 常 常

議	GI (50-7): to debate, to deliberate
	不思議 FUSHIGI (50-7): inconceivable, strange
149-13 　20	言 言 言 誹 誹 誹 誹 議 議 議

顔	*kao* (50-8): face
	顔色 *kaoiro*: complexion
181-9 　18	亠 立 立 产 彦 彦 顔 顔 顔

131

猫	*neko* (50-9): cat
	猫舌 *nekojita* (lit: cat's tongue): impossibility of eating or drinking something when hot
94-9　　12	ノ　 犭　犭　犭　犰　犰　猫　猫　猫

鼻	*hana* (50-11): nose
209-0　　14	′　冂　自　自　鼻　鼻　畠　畠　鼻　鼻

夢	*yume* (50-14), MU: dream
	悪夢 AKUMU: nightmare
36-10　　13	一　艹　芦　苗　茜　芦　夢　夢　夢

森	*mori* (50-14), SHIN: woods, forest
	森林 SHINRIN: the forests
75-8　　12	一　十　オ　木　术　森

区	<u>KU</u> (51-6): district, area
	千代田区 *chiyoda*KU (68-7): the Chiyoda quarter
23-2　　4	一　フ　ヌ　区

衆	SHŪ (51-10): large number, multiple 公衆電話 KŌSHŪDENWA (51-10): public telephone
143-6 12	′ ″ ⼾ ⾎ 血 岍 帠 衆 帠 衆

玉	*tama, -dama* (51-12): ball, sphere; jewel 十円玉 JŪ.EN*dama* (51-12): a 10-yen coin
96-0 5	一 丁 干 王 玉

巨	KYO (52-1): enormous, immense 巨大 KYODAI (52-1): enormous, huge
22-2 5	丨 厂 厂 戸 巨

網	*ami* (52-1): web, net
120-8 14	⼅ ⼁ 糸 紵 網 網 網 網 網

町	*machi* (52-4), CHŌ: assembly of houses: neighborhood, village, town 町立 CHŌRITSU: communal
102-2 7	丨 冂 冂 用 田 田 町

広	*hiro(i)* (52-5), KŌ (92-14): to be wide, broad 広場 *hiroba*: a square, plaza 広告 KŌKOKU (92-14): publicity, advertisement
53-2　　　5	` 亠 广 広 広

張	*ha(ru)* (52-5), CHŌ: to stick, to tighten 出張 SHUTCHŌ (89-4): business trip
57-8　　　11	フ フ 弓 引 引 弭 張 張 張

盛	*saka(n)* (52-7): prosperous, flourishing
108-6　　　11	ノ 厂 万 成 成 成 成 盛 盛

番	BAN (52-9): guard, surveillance; order 番地 BANCHI (61-5): a house number
102-7　　　12	丿 丷 立 平 来 来 番 番 番

橋	*hashi* (53-1), KYŌ: bridge 鉄橋 TEKKYŌ: metal bridge, iron bridge
75-12　　　16	十 木 朾 杧 桥 杯 桥 橋 橋

腸	CHŌ (53-8): intestine
130-9　　13	） 刀 月 胪 胪 胛 胛 胛 腸 腸

黄	*ki* (53-9): yellow 黄色 *ki.iro* (53-9): the yellow color
201-0　　11	一 艹 艹 芦 芍 带 莆 黄 黄

借	*ka(riru)* (54-1), SHAKU, SHAK- (76-12): to borrow 借金 SHAKKIN (76-12): debt, loan
9-8　　10	） イ 亻 仁 㑊 件 供 借 借

替	*ka(eru)*, *-ga(eru)* (54-3): to exchange, to replace 着替える *kigaeru* (54-3): change clothes
73-8　　12	一 二 チ 夫 㚇 㚈 替 替 替

哲	TETSU (54-4): clear 哲学 TETSUGAKU: philosophy
30-7　　10	一 十 才 扌 扩 折 折 折 哲 哲

雄	*o* (54-4): male, *end of masculine first name*
172-4　　12	一 ナ ナ ナ 左 ナ左 ナ左 ナ左 ナ隹 雄
規	KI (54-5): standard, model 規定 KITEI: rules, regulations
147-4　　11	一 二 ナ 夫 却 却 却 規 規
帽	BŌ (54-5): hat 帽子 BŌSHI (54-5): hat
50-9　　12	丨 冂 巾 忄 忄 忄 忄 忄 帽 帽
被	*kabu(ru)* (54-6): to wear as a hat
145-5　　10	` ラ ネ ネ ネ 衤 衤 衤 被 被
岩	*iwa* (54-8): rock, crag
46-5　　8	丨 屮 山 屵 屵 岩 岩 岩

競	KYŌ (54-8): emulation, competition 競争 KYŌSŌ (54-8): competition
117-15　20	ヽ ユ ウ 立 产 音 音 竟 竟 竟 競 競 競
勝	*ka(tsu)* (54-9), SHŌ: to win, to be victorious 勝利 SHŌRI: victory, triumph
19-10　12	） 月 月 月´ 肝 胖 脒 胖 勝 勝
危	*abuna(i)* (54-10), KI: to be dangerous 危険 KIKEN: danger, risk
26-4　6	ノ ク ク 产 户 危
砂	*suna* (54-12), SA: sand 砂漠 SABAKU: desert
112-4　9	一 ア 不 石 石 石´ 砂 砂 砂
背	*se* (54-13), HAI: the back 背広 *sebiro* (74-1): a man's suit 背景 HAIKEI: background
130-5　9	一 十 土 土` 北 北 背 背

付	*tsu(keru)* (54-ex. 4), *-zukeru* (80-1), FU: to link, to attach 片付ける *katazukeru* (80-1): to put in order, tidy up
9-3　　　5	ノ イ イ 付 付

去	KO, KYO (55-3): to leave, to be past 去年 KYO.NEN (55-3): last year
28-3　　　5	一 十 土 去 去

換	*ka(eru)* (55-8): to exchange, to replace 乗り換える *norikaeru* (55-8): to change (trains, subway…)
64-9　　　12	一 十 扌 扩 护 捇 捇 換 換

船	*fune* (55-9), SEN: boat 汽船 KISEN: steamship
137-5　　　11	ノ 厂 力 力 舟 舟 舟 舟 船 船

屈	KUTSU (55-11): to crouch, to bend, to submit 退屈 TAIKUTSU (55-11): tedium, ennui, monotony
44-5　　　8	一 コ 尸 尸 屈 屈 屈 屈

歴	REKI (57-title): time going by 歴史 REKISHI (57-title): history
77-10　　14	一 厂 厈 厈 厤 麻 麻 歷 歷 歷

史	SHI (57-title): chronicles, history 科学史 KAGAKUSHI (87-ex. 4): history of science
30-2　　5	丶 口 口 口 史 史

奈	(A) 奈良 *nara* (57-1): Nara
37-5 *　　8	一 ナ 大 太 杰 李 奈 奈

良	*i(i)*, *yo(i)*, RYŌ: to be good 良心 RYŌSHIN: conscience, scruple (A) 奈良 *nara* (57-1): Nara
138-1　　7	丶 ㇇ ㇕ ㇕ 自 良 良

回	*mawa(ru)*: to turn, to pivot; *mawa(ri)* (57-3), KAI (58-13): turn, time 今回 KONKAI (58-13): this time
31-3　　6	丨 冂 冂 冋 回 回

畑	*hatake* (57-4): field
102-4 9	丶 ⺍ ⺌ 火 灯 炉 畑 畑

寺	*tera* (57-4), JI (57-5): Buddhist temple 東大寺 TŌDAIJI (57-5): Tōdaji Buddhist Temple
41-3 6	一 十 土 圡 寺 寺

法	HŌ (57-5), -PŌ (88-5): rule, principle; method, means 法律 HŌRITSU: law, legislation 文法 BUNPŌ: grammar
85-5 8	丶 丶 氵 汀 汁 泫 法 法

隆	RYŪ (57-5): prosper 興隆 KŌRYŪ: rise, prosperity
170-8 11	⻖ 彐 阝 阝 阽 阼 陜 陜 陜 降 隆

薬	*kusuri* (81-5), YAKU (57-5): medicine, medication 薬品 YAKUHIN (81-8): medication
140-3 16	一 艹 艹 苎 苩 草 薄 薄 薬 薬

師	SHI (57-5): master, teacher
50-7　　10	´ 亻 ⺊ ⻊ 𠂤 自 𠂤 𠂤 師 師

唐	kara-, TŌ (57-5): China, Chinese things, the Chinese Tang Dynasty 唐画 TŌGA: Chinese-style painting
30-7　　10	` 亠 广 户 庐 庐 庐 唐 唐

招	mane(ku), SHŌ (57-5): to invite 招待 SHŌTAI: an invitation
64-5　　8	一 十 扌 扚 扪 招 招 招

転	koro(bu) (71-ex. 3), TEN (57-7): to roll, to tumble 自転車 JITENSHA (57-7): bicycle
159-4　　11	一 厂 百 亘 車 軒 軒 転 転

泊	to(maru) (57-9), HAKU, -PAKU (86-10): to spend a night, to make a stop 一泊 IPPAKU (86-10): a one night stop/break 二泊 NIHAKU: a two nights (3 days) stop/break
85-5　　8	` 丶 氵 氵 汐 泊 泊 泊

選	*era(bu)* (65-title), SEN (58-title): to choose 選び方 *erabikata* (65-13): manner of choice 選手 SENSHU: athlete, champion
162-12　15	｀ ｺ ㄹ 己 邑 巽 巽 巽 巽 選
挙	KYO (58-title): project, action 選挙 SENKYO (58-title): elections
64-6　　10	｀ ｀ ｀ ｀ ｨ ｨ 兴 兴 尚 尚 挙
旗	*hata* (58-3): flag
70-10　14	ｰ 亠 方 斺 斺 斺 旆 旗 旗
繰	*ku(ru)* (58-6): to roll up in a coil, to turn a page 繰り返す *kurikaesu* (58-6): to repeat, to say again
120-13　19	⟨ ㄠ ㄠ 糸 糸 紗 紗 繰 繰 繰
返	*kae(su)* (58-6), HEN (61-title): to re-send, to give back 返事 HENJI (61-title): answer, reply
162-4　　7	ｰ 厂 厉 反 反 返 返

運	UN (58-7): destiny, luck; transport 運命 UNMEI: destiny 運転 UNTEN (97-7): driving (a vehicle)
162-9　12	丶 一 一 宀 冖 冃 冒 冒 軍 運

候	KŌ (58-8): season, weather 候補 KŌHO (58-8): candidate
9-8　10	亻 仆 仆 伫 伫 伫 俟 候 候

補	*ogina(u)*, HO (58-8): to assist, to supplement 補助 HOJO: help, assistance
145-7　12	丶 ブ ネ ネ 衤 衤 衤 袘 補 補

障	SHŌ (59-title): to interfere, to hinder 故障 KOSHŌ (59-title): breakdown
170-11　14	フ ろ ß ß ß ß 陪 陪 障 障

竹	*take* (59-2): bamboo 竹林 *takebayashi*: bamboo grove
118-0　6	ノ ト ケ ケ 竹 竹

洗	*ara(u)*, SEN (59-2): to wash
	洗濯 SENTAKU (62-7): (to do the) laundry
85-6 9	` ` シ シ シ 汀 汁 汼 泮 洗

濯	TAKU (59-2): to pour on, to rince
	洗濯機 SENTAKUKI (59-2): washing machine
85-14 17	シ シ シ 浬 浬 浬 渾 渾 濯

掃	SŌ (59-7): to sweep, to brush
	掃除 SŌJI (74-9): cleaning
64-8 11	一 十 才 扫 扫 护 护 掃 掃

除	JI (59-7): to exclude, to remove
	掃除機 SŌJIKI (59-7): vacuum cleaner
170-7 10	´ ³ ß ß' ßヽ 阶 除 除

蔵	ZŌ (59-10): storage, warehouse
	冷蔵庫 REIZŌKO (59-10): refrigerator
140-12 15	艹 芦 芹 芹 芹 芦 蕆 蔵 蔵 蔵

奥	*oku* (59-11): inside, the back 奥さん *okusan* (59-11): wife; Mrs…
37-9　　12	´ ⼁ ⼌ 冇 向 向 甪 奥 奥 奥
抜	*nu(ku)*: to extract, *nu(keru)* (59-11): to fall, to miss
64-4　　7	⼀ ⼗ ⼧ 扌 扩 扷 抜
具	GU (59-12): utensil, tool 器具 KIGU (59-12): instrument, device
12-6　　8	⼁ ⼌ 目 且 且 具 具
解	KAI (59-12): explanation, understanding 解決 KAIKETSU: solution
148-6　　13	´ ⼍ 勹 角 角 角 觧 觧 觧 解 解
是	ZE (59-ex. 3): right, justice 是非 ZEHI (59-ex. 3): absolutely, by any means
72-5　　9	⼁ ⼌ 日 旦 早 早 昦 是

幹	*miki*, KAN (60-title): trunk
	新幹線 SHINKANSEN (60-title): the Shinkansen
51-10 13	十 古 古 卓 卓 卓′ 卓ヘ 幹ヘ 幹ヘ 幹

州	SHŪ (60-1): province, state
	九州 KYŪSHŪ (60-1): the island of Kyūshū
47-3 6	′ ′ ′ 小 州 州 州

孫	*mago* (60-1), SON: grandchild, grandchildren
	子孫 SHISON: descendants, posterity
39-7 10	ア 了 子 子 子′ 孖 弪 孫 孫 孫

比	*kura(beru)* (60-5), HI: to compare
	比較 HIKAKU: comparison
81-0 4	ー ヒ ヒ′ 比

窓	*mado* (60-8): window
	窓口 *madoguchi*: counter, (ticket) window
116-6 11	′ ′′ 宀 灾 灾 空 空 穼 窓 窓

念	NEN (60-8): thought, idea
	残念 ZANNEN (60-8): regrettable, disappointing
61-4　　8	ノ 人 今 今 念 念 念

房	BŌ (60-9): room, house
	冷房 REIBŌ (60-9): air-conditioned
63-4　　8	一 ラ ヨ 戸 戸 戸 房 房

確	*tashi(ka)* (60-10), KAKU (61-9): sure, certain
	確実 KAKUJITSU: certainty, authenticity
112-10　15	一 丁 石 矿 矿 矿 矿 砕 碏 確

蒸	*mu(su)* (60-10): to steam, to give off steam
	蒸し暑い *mushiatsui* (60-10): to be hot and humid
140-10　13	一 艹 艹 芋 芽 茅 蒸 蒸 蒸 蒸

| 涼 | *suzushi(i)* (60-10): to be cool (weather) |
| 85-8　　11 | ` `` ` ` 汁 汁 泸 泸 涼 涼 |

寒	*samu(i)* (60-10): to be cold
40-9　　12	⼀ ⼩ ⼧ ⼧ ⼧ ⼧ ⼧ ⼧ 寒 寒
椅	I (60-11): chair 椅子 ISU (60-11): chair
75-8*　　12	⼀ ⼗ ⽊ ⽊ ⽊ ⽊ ⽊ 椅 椅
浜	*hama* (60-11): the beach 浜辺 *hamabe*: beach, bank 横浜 *yokohama* (60-11): Yokohama
85-7　　10	⼀ ⼀ ⼫ ⼫ ⼫ ⼫ 泸 泸 浜 浜
阪	*saka* (60-13): slope 大阪 *oosaka* (60-13): Ōsaka
170-4*　　7	⼀ ⼀ ⼩ ⼩ ⼩ 阪 阪

受	*u(keru)* (61-1): to receive 受け取る *uketoru* (61-1): to receive
29-6　　8	⼀ ⼀ ⼩ ⼩ ⼩ ⼩ 受 受

送	*oku(ru)* (61-2), SŌ (92-4): to send, to deliver 見送る *miokuru* (78-12): to accompany, to take back 放送 HŌSŌ (92-11): broadcast
162-6　　9	丶　丶丶　䒑　兰　关　关　送　送

封	FŪ (61-4): stamp, mark; HŌ: fief 封建 HŌKEN: Feudalism 封建時代 HŌKENJIDAI: Feudal era
41-6　　9	一　十　土　圭　丰　圭　封　封

筒	TŌ (61-4): tube 封筒 FŪTŌ (61-4): envelope
118-6　　12	丿　ト　ケ　竹　竹　筧　筒　筒　筒

北	*kita* (61-5), HOKU, HOK- (97-6): north 北部 HOKUBU: the north part 北海道 HOKKAIDŌ (97-6): Hokkaidō Island
21-3　　5	一　十　北　北

銭	SEN (62-title): one sen (a cent of yen) 銭湯 SENTŌ (62-title): public baths
167-6　　14	丿　人　牟　余　金　鈩　銭　銭　銭

湯	*yu* (62-4), TŌ (62-title): hot water
85-9　　12	` ` ⺡ 沪 沪 沪 湯 湯 湯

宿	SHUKU (62-1), JUKU (65-2): post house 民宿 MINSHUKU (75-13): a guesthouse 新宿 SHINJUKU (65-2): Shinjuku
40-8　　11	` ⼧ 宀 宀 宁 宵 宿 宿 宿

呂	RO (62-1): vertebral column (A) 風呂場 *furoba* (66-10): bath/shower room
30-4 *　7	` 口 口 呂 呂 呂 呂

派	HA, -PA (62-4): group, faction 派生 HASEI: derivation 立派 RIPPA (62-4): exceptional, magnificent
85-6　　9	` ` ⺡ 氵 沪 沂 沂 派 派

槽	SŌ: vat, tank *湯槽 *yubune* (62-4): bath
75-11　15	一 十 才 木 杧 柿 柿 槽 槽

深	*fuka(i)* (62-4): to be deep; *fuka(mi)* (96-11): depth
85-8 11	丶 冫 氵 氵 氵 氵 沪 沪 深 深 深

満	MAN (62-5): fullness 満員 MAN.IN (62-5): full, complete
85-9 12	氵 氵 汢 洪 洪 満 満 満 満

浸	*tsuka(ru)* (62-5): to be immersed
85-7 10	氵 氵 浔 浔 浔 浔 浸 浸

設	*mō(keru)*, SETSU (62-6): to establish, to found, to organize 建設 KENSETSU: construction
149-4 11	丶 言 言 言 言 訁 訳 設 設

備	BI (62-6): to be provided with 設備 SETSUBI (62-6): accommodation, installation
9-10 12	亻 亻 俨 俨 俨 俨 備 備 備

玄	GEN (62-7): mystery 玄関 GEN.KAN (62-7): entry, vestibule
95-0 5	` 一 亠 玄 玄

裸	*hadaka* (62-8): naked, nude
145-8 13	` フ ネ ネ ネ 衤 衵 衵 裡 裸

雑	ZATSU, ZAK-, ZAS- (64-title), ZAP-: diverse, miscellaneous 雑音 ZATSUON: noise 雑貨 ZAKKA: diverse objects 雑費 ZAPPI: diverse fees
172-6 14	ノ 九 卒 杂 刹 刹′ 新 新 雑

誌	SHI (64-title): documents 雑誌 ZASSHI (64-title): a magazine
149-7 14	` 言 言 言 計 計 許 誌 誌

勉	BEN (64-1): to work 勉強 BENKYŌ (64-1) study, work
19-8 10	ク 勹 夕 宀 宀 宀 免 免 勉

個	KO (64-4): individual 個人 KOJIN (64-4): an individual, a private person
9-8　　　10	イ 们 们 佣 価 個 個 個 個

読	*yo(mu)* (64-5): to read 読み方 *yomikata*: way of reading, pronunciation
149-7　　　14	、 言 言 言 計 計 計 読 読 読

記	KI (64-8): story, narration, memory 記念 KI.NEN: souvenir, commemoration
149-3　　　10	、 言 言 言 言 言 記 記 記

農	NŌ (64-11): agriculture 農場 NŌJŌ (97-6): farm 農家 NŌKA: a farmhouse
161-6　　　13	、 口 曲 曲 曹 芦 芦 農 農 農

面	*omote*, MEN (64-11): face, surface, exterior 面白い *omoshiroi* (82-4): to be interesting 方面 HŌMEN (64-11): direction field
176-0　　　9	一 ア ア 币 而 而 面 面

構	KŌ (65-5): to establish, to install 構造 KŌZŌ: structure
75-10　　14	木　木　柯　槽　槽　構　構　構　構
型	*kata*, *-gata* (65-6): type, model 小型 *kogata* (65-6): small size
32-6　　9	一　二　チ　开　开　刑　刑　型　型
御	GO (65-7): *prefix for high degree* 御案内 GO.ANNAI (94-3): greeting of an important person
60-9　　11	彳　彳　彳　行　行　御　御　御　御
覧	RAN (67-7): to see 御覧下さい GORAN *kudasai* (65-7): please have a look at (high degree)
147-10　　17	｜　厂　厂　严　臣　臣　臣　臣　臣　臤　瞥　覧
値	*ne* (65-8): price, value 値段 *ne*DAN (65-8): price
9-8　　10	ノ　イ　イ　仁　仕　仕　估　値　値　値

軽	*karu(i)* (65-12): to be light
159-5　　12	一 ｢ 戸 百 亘 車 軒 輊 軽 軽

石	*ishi* (66-1), SEKI: stone, rock 石油 SEKIYU: petroleum
112-0　　5	一 ｢ 不 石 石

井	*i* (66-1): well 井戸 *ido*: well
7-2　　4	一 二 ヺ 井

震	*furu(eru)*, SHIN (66-3): to tremble, to quake 地震 JISHIN (66-3): earthquake
173-7　　15	一 厂 币 乕 雫 雫 震 震 震 震 震

純	JUN (66-4): purity, innocence 純日本風 JUNNIHONFŪ (66-4): purely Japanese
120-4　　10	く 幺 幺 糸 糸 糽 紅 紅 純

盆	BON (66-6): plateau, Lantern Festival 盆景 BONKEI: miniature garden
108-4　　9	ノ 八 今 今 分 分 盆 盆 盆
栽	SAI (66-6): to plant 盆栽 BONSAI (66-6): baby trees, bonsai
75-6　　10	一 十 土 圭 圭 丰 未 栽 栽 栽
数	*kazu*, SŪ (66-9): number, digit 数学 SŪGAKU (92-10): mathematics
66-9　　13	゛ 半 米 半 娄 娄 娄 娄 数 数
応	Ō (66-10): to subscribe to, to agree to, to correspond to 応用 ŌYŌ: practical application
61-3　　7	' 亠 广 广 広 応 応
接	SETSU (66-10), SET- (69-5): to be in contact, to receive 応接 ŌSETSU (66-10): a reception
64-8　　11	一 十 才 扩 护 护 接 接 接 接

堂	DŌ (66-10): sanctuary; hall, large room
	食堂 SHOKUDŌ (66-10): dining room, dining hall
32-8　　11	丶 ⺍ ⺌ ⺍ 尚 尚 堂 堂 堂

式	SHIKI (66-10): rite, style, method
	日本式 NIHONSHIKI (66-10): Japanese style, Japanese manner
56-3　　6	一 ニ テ 弍 式 式

準	JUN (66-11): to correspond to, to be conformed to
	準備 JUNBI (66-11): preparation
85-10　　13	シ シ 氵 汁 汁 汁 淮 淮 淮 準

| 娘 | *musume* (66-ex. 3): girl, young girl |
| 38-7　　10 | し 女 女 女' 妒 娘 娘 娘 娘 |

無	MU (66-ex. 3), BU (86-3): nothing, *negation*
	無理 MURI (66-ex. 3): vain, useless, impossible 無事 BUJI: safe and sound, secure
86-8　　12	丿 ⺅ 缶 缶 缶 無 無 無

詳	*kuwa(shii)* (66-ex. 4), SHŌ: to be detailed
149-6　13	亠 亠 言 言 言 訁 評 詳 詳
載	*no(ru)* (66. ex. 4): to figure, to be mentioned
159-6　13	一 一 二 丰 亘 車 載 載 載
富	FU (67-title): riches, wealth 富国 FUKOKU: rich and powerful country
40-9　12	丶 宀 宀 宀 宀 富 宮 宮 富 富

士	SHI (67-title): warrior 富士山 FUJISAN (67-title): Mount Fuji
33-0　3	一 十 士
遍	HEN, -PEN (67-4): time 普遍 FUHEN: pervasive, universal 一遍 IPPEN (67-4): one time
162-9　12	一 ㄱ ㅋ 尸 尸 肩 肩 扁 漏 遍

伊	(A) 伊豆 *izu* (67-5): the Izu peninsula
9-4　　　6	ノ 亻 亻゛ 伊 伊 伊 伊

豆	*mame*, ZU (67-5): bean, pea
151-0　　　7	一 𠂉 𠮷 豆 豆 豆 豆

掛	*ka(keru)* (67-5): to hang 出掛ける *dekakeru* (67-5): to leave one's house for a moment
64-8　　　11	一 十 扌 扌 扩 扩 挂 挂 挂 掛 掛

葬	SŌ (67-7): to bury 葬式 SŌSHIKI (67-7): funeral
140-9　　　12	一 艹 艹 艿 艻 芴 芴 茐 菀 葬

霊	REI (67-7): soul, spirit 霊園 REIEN (67-7): cemetery park
173-7　　　15	一 厂 戸 币 雫 雪 雪 霊 霊

159

墓	*haka* (67-8), BO (67-8): tomb 墓地 BOCHI (67-8): cemetery
32-10　　13	一　艹　苩　苩　莒　莫　莫　莫　墓　墓
仮	KA (80-ex. 1), -GA (67-ex. 1): provisional, temporary 仮定 KATEI: hypothesis, supposition
9-4　　6	ノ　イ　仁　仾　仮　仮
械	KAI (67-ex.4): machine 機械 KIKAI (67-ex. 4): machine
75-7　　11	十　才　木　朾　杉　杉　栎　械　械　械

皇	KŌ (68-title), Ō: emperor 皇居 KŌKYO (68-7): Imperial Palace 天皇 TENNŌ (68-5): the Emperor
106-4　　9	ノ　イ　宀　白　白　自　皁　皇　皇
止	*to(maru)* (68-1), SHI (82-2): to be stopped, to be interrupted; *to(meru)*, SHI: to stop, to interrupt 中止 CHŪSHI: cease, interruption
77-0　　4	丨　ト　止　止

陛	HEI (68-5): steps of the throne 両陛下 RYŌHEIKA (68-9): Their (two) Majesties
170-7　　10	⁷ ³ ㇡ ㇏ ㇏ ㇏ ㇏ ㇏ ㇏ 陛

列	<u>RETSU</u>, RES- (68-7): line, file 列車 RESSHA (68-7): a train
18-4　　6	一 ア 歹 歹 列 列

后	KŌ (68-8): after, following 皇后 KŌGŌ (68-8): the Empress
30-3　　6	⁄ 厂 ㇆ 斤 后 后

姿	*sugata* (68-10), SHI: form, appearance, figure 姿勢 SHISEI: attitude, posture, position
38-6　　9	丶 ⼆ ⼅ ⼎ ⼎ ⼎ 次 姿 姿

宮	KYŪ (68-10): palace 宮廷 KYŪTEI: the Court
40-7　　10	丶 丷 宀 宀 宀 宮 宮 宮 宮 宮

参	*mai(ru)* (86-10), SAN (68-10): to go (high degree: I) 参加 SANKA: to take part, to participate 参加者 SANKASHA: participant
28-6　　8	⺊ ⺕ ⺕ 夬 失 叅 参 参

賀	GA (68-10): congratulations, compliments 年賀 NENGA: new year's good wishes
154-5　　12	フ カ カ 加 加 加 智 智 智 賀

将	SHŌ (68-11): general of an army; soon 将来 SHŌRAI (94-11): future
41-7　　10	｜ ⺉ ⺔ ⺔ 扌 护 护 护 将 将

軍	GUN (68-11): army 将軍 SHŌGUN (68-11): the Shogun, the supreme general of the military
159-2　　9	′ ⼍ ⼍ 尸 冒 冒 軍 軍 軍

城	*shiro* (68-11), JŌ: castle 城下町 JŌKA*machi*: walled city
32-6　　9	一 十 土 圠 圹 圻 城 城 城

甥	*oi* (69-1): nephew 甥御さん *oiGOsan* (69-2): your nephew
100-7*　　12	ノ　ト　牛　生　甥　甥　甥　甥　甥

済	SAI, -ZAI (69-1): to finish, to avoid 経済 KEIZAI (69-1): economy, finance
85-8　　11	シ　汀　汀　汀　汸　済　済　済　済

性	SEI (69-5): gender, nature, sex 性格 SEIKAKU: character, personality 社交性 SHAKŌSEI (69-5): of social temperament
61-5　　8	丶　ハ　忄　忄　忙　忓　性　性

想	SŌ (69-5): thought, idea 理想 RISŌ (69-5): ideal
61-9　　13	一　十　才　木　札　机　相　相　想　想

条	JŌ (69-6): clause, article 条約 JŌYAKU: treaty, agreement, convention
75-3　　7	ノ　ク　タ　冬　冬　条

件	KEN (69-6): subject, case 条件 JŌKEN (69-6): conditions
9-4　　　6	ノ　イ　イ　仁　仁　件
連	*tsura(naru)*, REN (69-11): to be linked to, to join to; *tsureru* (82-5): to accompany 国際連盟 KOKUSAIRENSEI: the United Nations
162-7　　10	一　ア　戸　百　亘　車　軍　連　連
絡	RAKU (69-11): to roll around, to stick to 連絡 RENRAKU (69-11): link, communication, contact
120-6　　12	く　幺　幺　糸　糸　糽　絡　絡　絡
億	<u>OKU</u> (69-ex. 5): 1,0000,0000; one hundred million 九億円 KYŪ.OKUEN (69-ex. 5): 9,0000,0000 yen
9-13　　15	ノ　イ　彳　仁　佇　倍　倍　億　億

振	*fu(ru)* (71-9): to shake, to stir
64-7　　10	一　十　扌　扩　扩　护　拆　振　振

袖	*sode* (71-9): sleeves 振り袖 *furisode* (71-9): long-sleeved kimono
145-5*　10	` ラ ㇠ ネ ネ 袟 初 袖 袖

我	GA (71-10): oneself, egotism 我慢 GAMAN (71-10): patience, self-mastery
62-3　7	´ ⼆ 千 手 我 我 我

慢	MAN (71-10): to play with, to scorn, to be lazy 自慢 JIMAN (72-4): vanity, pride
61-11　14	' ⺌ 忄 忄 忸 慢 慢 慢 慢

沢	*sawa, -zawa* (72-4): marsh, swamp
85-4　7	` ㇀ 氵 汀 沪 沢 沢

君	*kimi* (75-3): you (low degree); -KUN (72-4): *after a masculine name* (low degree)
30-4　7	⼁ ㇕ ㇍ ㇌ 尹 尹 君 君

72

雪	*yuki* (72-5): snow 雪景色 *yuki*GESHIKI (72-5): landscape with snow
173-3 11	
景	KEI (85-9), KE (75-1), -GE (72-5): view, scene 風景 FŪKEI (85-9): scene, view, landscape
72-8 12	
又	*mata* (72-6): anew
29-0 2	

73

支	SHI (73-3): branch, support 支度 SHITAKU (73-3): preparation
65-0 4	
疲	*tsuka(reru)* (75-1): to be tired; *tsuka(re)* (73-3): tiredness, fatigue
104-5 10	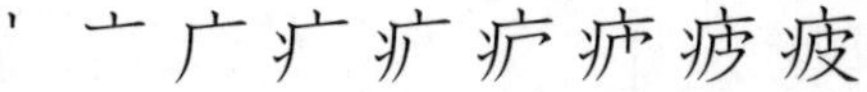

沸	*wa(ku)*: to boil; *wa(kasu)* (73-7): to bring to a boil
85-5　　8	丶 丶 氵 沪 沪 沪 沸 沸

| 睡 | SUI (73-9): to sleep |
	睡眠 SUIMIN (79-9): sleep
109-8　　13	丨 冂 目 目 肝 肝 肝 睡 睡

| 体 | *karada* (73-9), TAI: the body |
| | 大体 DAITAI: generally, in general |
	全体 ZENTAI: total, totality, entire
9-5　　7	丿 亻 亻 什 什 休 体

噂	*uwasa* (73-14): rumor
30-12*　　15	口 咕 咕 喈 喈 喈 喧 噂 噂

| 羅 | RA (74-1): silk |
	一張羅 ITCHŌRA (74-1): only presentable outfit
122-14　　19	丶 冖 罒 罒 罒 罗 罗 罗 羅 羅 羅

74

鳴	*na(ku)*: to make hear one's cry (for animals or insects); *na(rasu)* (74-1): to resonate, ring
196-3　14	丶 口 口′ 叮 叮 咆 咱 鳴 鳴 鳴
整	*totono(u)* (74-7), SEI: to be in order; *totono(eru)*: to put in order 整理 SEIRI: arrangement, put in order
66-12　16	一 一 宀 束 敕 敕 敕 整 整 整
蕎	KYŌ (74-9): buckwheat * 蕎麦 *soba* (74-9): buckwheat noodles, soba
140-12*　15	艹 艹 芏 芦 芖 莽 萕 蕎 蕎
拝	*oga(mu)* (74-9): to adore, to venerate, to worship
64-5　8	一 寸 扌 扩 扩 拝 拝
晦	* 晦日 *misoka*: the last day of the month * 大晦日 *oomisoka* (74-11): the last day of the year
72-7*　10	丨 冂 日 日′ 旷 旷 昕 晦 晦

168

慣	KAN (74-11): to get used to, to be familiar with 習慣 SHŪKAN (74-11): habit, custom
61-11 14	` ' ' 忄 忄 忄 忄 忄 忄 慣 慣 慣

苦	*kuru(shii)*, KU (74-12): annoying, difficult 苦労 KURŌ (74-12): trouble, effort
140-5 8	一 十 艹 芐 芐 苦 苦 苦

労	RŌ (74-12): labor, trouble 労働 RŌDŌ: manual labor 労働者 RŌDŌSHA: manual laborer, worker
19-5 7	` '' ''' '''' 丷 労 労

様	*sama* (74-12): *after a person's name* (high degree), *or in expressions*; YŌ: manner, sort 様子 YŌSU: situation, circumstances
75-10 14	一 十 木 栌 栌 栌 様 様 様

澄	*su(mu)* (75-2): to be clear, to be transparent
85-12 15	氵 氵 氵 氵 浐 浐 澄 澄 澄

飯		*meshi* (75-3), HAN (82-ex. 4): cooked rice; meal 晩飯 BAN*meshi* (75-3): dinner 晩御飯 BANGOHAN (82-ex. 4): dinner
184-4	12	ノ 𠆢 𠆢 今 今 仒 食 食 飣 飣 飯 飯
枕		*makura* (75-4): pillow
75-4*	8	一 十 才 木 木 杓 枋 枕
嫌		*kira(u)* (75-7), KEN, GEN (87-12): to hate; *kirai* (81-6), *iya* (93-5): hateful 機嫌 KIGEN (87-12): disposition, mood
38-10	13	〈 夂 女 女 女 女 妒 姄 婷 婷 嫌 嫌
南		*minami* (75-8), NAN: south 南部 NANBU: the southern part
24-7	9	一 十 冂 冂 冂 冇 南 南 南
斜		SHA (75-9): slanted 斜面 SHAMEN (75-9): a slope, incline
68-7	11	ノ 𠆢 亼 亽 余 余 余 余 斜 斜

75

途	TO (75-13): way, path 途中 TOCHŪ (75-13): en route, on the way
162-7 10	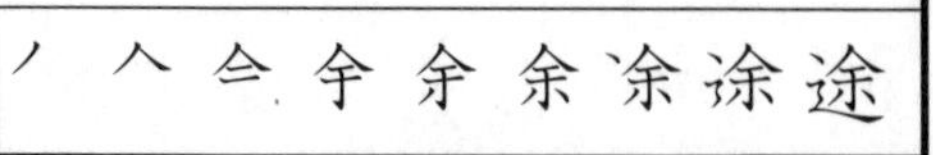

暖	*atata(kai)* (75-ex. 3), DAN: to be warm 暖房 DANBŌ: central heating
72-9 13	

76

隙	*suki* (76-1): time, space 隙間 *sukima* (76-1): crack, fissure
170-10* 13	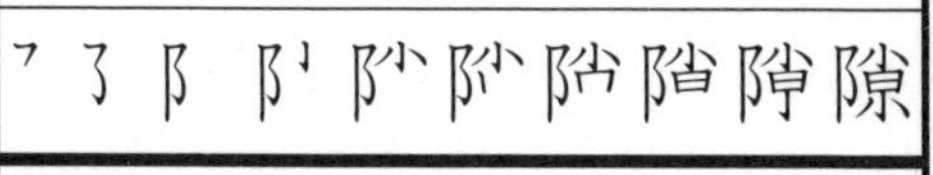

湖	*mizuumi*, KO (76-2): lake 山中湖 *yamanaka*KO (76-2): Lake Yamanaka
85-9 12	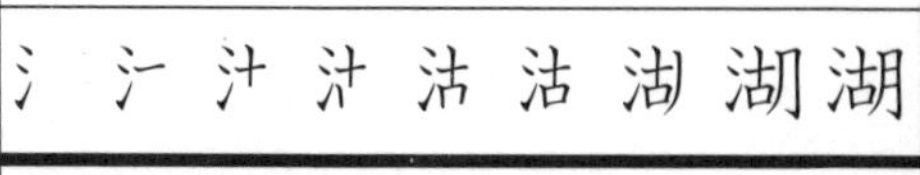

荘	SŌ (76-2): hamlet, villa 別荘 BESSŌ (76-2): villa
140-6 9	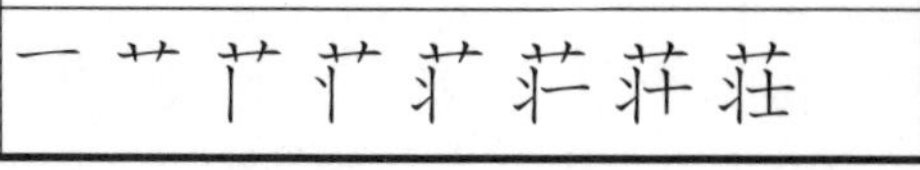

避	*sa(keru)*, HI (76-2): to avoid, to keep from doing sth
	避暑 HISHO (76-2): the act of avoiding heat by leaving the city
162-13　16	⁊ 尸 尸 尸ʾ 尸ʾ 辟 辟 辟 辟 避

稿	KŌ (76-2): manuscript, copy
	原稿 GENKŌ (76-2): manuscript
115-10　15	⸃ ⸊ 千 禾 秆 秆 秆 稿 稿

| 鰐 | *wani* (76-3): crocodile |
| 195-9　20 | ⁄ 勹 ⼑ 名 角 鱼 魚 魛 魛 鰐 鰐 鰐 |

指	*yubi* (76-3), SHI: finger
	指導 SHIDŌ: leadership, guidance
64-6　9	一 十 扌 扩 托 托 指 指 指

輪	*wa* (76-3): circle, wheel
	指輪 *yubiwa* (76-3): ring
159-8　15	一 日 亘 車 車ʾ 軩 軩 軩 輪 輪

界	KAI (76-6): circle, world 世界 SEKAI (76-6): the world, the Earth
102-4　　9	丿 冂 冂 田 甼 界 界 界 界

周	SHŪ (76-6): circuit, circumference, tour 一周 ISSHŪ (76-6): one round, a tour
30-5　　8	丿 冂 刀 円 円 周 周 周

踊	*odo(ru)* (76-10): to dance
157-7　　14	口 卩 卩 卩 足 趵 趵 踊 踊 踊

辞	JI (78-6): word, expression 辞儀 JIGI (78-6): bow, salute
160-6　　13	丿 二 千 舌 舌 舌 舌 辞 辞

儀	GI (78-6): ceremony, ritual 礼儀 REIGI: politeness, etiquette
9-13　　15	亻 亻 亻 俨 俨 俨 俨 儀 儀 儀

政	SEI (78-7): government 政治 SEIJI (88-5): politics
66-4 8	一 丁 下 正 正 正 政 政

府	FU (78-7): administrative bureau 政府 SEIFU (78-7): government
53-5 8	丶 亠 广 广 广 庐 府 府

科	KA (78-7): department, branch, family 科学 KAGAKU (78-7): science 理科 RIKA (94-9): the technical sciences
115-4 9	一 二 千 禾 禾 禾 禾 科 科

研	KEN (78-7): to polish, to sharpen 研究 KENKYŪ (78-7): research
112-4 9	一 厂 丆 石 石 石 矿 研 研

究	KYŪ (78-7): extreme, the highest rank 研究所 KENKYŪJO: research institute, graduate school
116-2 7	丶 宀 宀 宀 究 究 究

頃	*koro* (78-9), *-goro* (83-1): towards, around (+ time notion) あの頃 *anokoro* (78-9): towards that moment この頃 *konogoro* (83-1): towards this moment, currently
181-2* 11	一　ヒ　ヒ゛　ヒ゜　ヒ゜　頃　頃　頃　頃　頃

迷	*mayo(u)*, MEI (79-5), MAI (97-1): to be lost, to doubt 迷路 MEIRO (79-5): maze 迷子 MAIGO (97-1): missing child
162-6 9	丶　丷　丷　半　米　米　米　迷　迷

勢	SEI, ZEI (79-7): energy, power 勢力 SEIRYOKU: authority, power, influence 大勢 *oo*ZEI (79-7): large number (of people)
19-11 13	一　十　士　夫　坴　坴丿　坴丸　執　執　勢　勢

改	*arata(meru)*, KAI (79-8): to correct, to improve, to change, to examine 改札口 KAISATSU*guchi* (79-8): ticket window (in subway)
66-3 7	フ　コ　己'　己ト　改　改

札	<u>SATSU</u> (79-8): *measure word for ticket-like objects*, bank bill 五千円札 GOSEN.ENSATSU (88-4): a 500-yen bill
75-1 5	一　十　才　木　札

示	*shime(su)*, SHI, JI (79-12): to indicate, to show 表示 HYŌJI (79-12): indication, expression
113-0 5	一 二 〒 示 示
板	*ita*, HAN, -BAN (79-12): plank, board 表示板 HYŌJIBAN (79-12): sign, information board
75-4 8	一 十 才 木 机 杭 板 板
盲	*mekura*, MŌ (70-13): blind 色盲 SHIKIMŌ (79-13): color-blind
109-3 8	` 亠 亡 亡 盲 盲 盲 盲
計	*haka(ru)*, KEI (79-ex. 1): to measure 時計 *to*KEI (79-ex. 1): watch, clock
149-2 9	` 亠 言 言 言 言 言 計

片	*kata* (80-1): one (of a pair) 片足 *kata.ashi* (99-9): one foot
91-0 4	ノ ﾉ 广 片

蒲	FU (80-3): birch 蒲団 FUTON (80-3): mattress, futon
140-10*　13	一　艹　芦　芦　芦　芦　蒲　蒲
団	TON (80-3), DAN (89-11): group, troup, organization 団子 DANGO (89-11): rice dumpling 団体 DANTAI: company, association
31-3　　6	丨　冂　闩　闬　団　団
机	*tsukue* (80-4): table, desk
75-2　　6	一　十　才　木　朾　机
菜	SAI (80-7): vegetables 野菜 YASAI (80-7): vegetables
140-8　　11	一　艹　艹　芯　芯　苙　苹　茟　菜
糖	TŌ (80-7): sugar 砂糖 SATŌ (80-7): powder sugar
119-10　16	丷　半　米　籵　籵　籵　粐　糖　糖

80

余	YO (80-10): remainder, surplus 余計 YOKEI: superfluous, useless, extraneous
9-5 7	
裕	YŪ (80-10): abundant, fertile 余裕 YOYŪ (80-10): spare (time, room…)
145-7 12	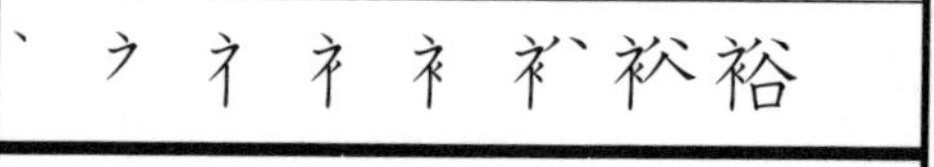
伝	*tsuta(eru)*, DEN: to transmit, to communicate * 手伝う *tetsudau* (80-14): to help 伝記 DENKI: biography
9-4 6	

81

邪	JA (83-9): injustice, evil * 風邪 *kaze* (81-title): a common cold
163-5 8	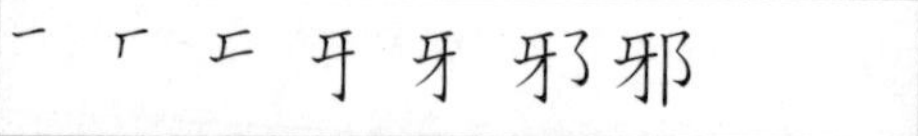
熱	*atsu(i)* (93-ex. 1), -NETSU, NES-: to be hot (to touch); <u>NETSU</u> (81-3): fever 熱心 NESSHIN: enthusiasm, passion
86-11 15	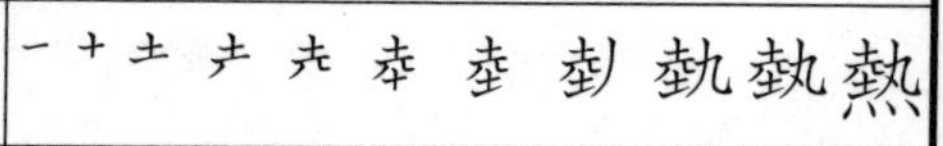

化	KA (81-8): to transform, to convert 化学 KAGAKU (81-8): chemistry
21-2　　4	ノ イ イ′ 化
抗	KŌ (81-8): to resist, to fight 抗生 KŌSEI (81-8): antibiotic
64-4　　7	一 十 才 扌′ 扩 扩 抗
鍼	*hari* (81-8): acupuncture needle
167-9*　17	入 ㅗ 午 牟 金 金 釗 釘 鋮 鍼 鍼
圧	ATSU (81-8): pressure 気圧 KI.ATSU: air pressure, atmospheric pressure
32-2　　5	一 厂 厈 圧 圧
漢	KAN (81-8): the Chinese Han Dynasty, China, Chinese 漢字 KANJI (99-8): Chinese writing, Chinese character
85-10　13	丶 氵 汀 汁 芦 芦 湛 漢 漢

徒	TO (82-1): group 生徒 SEITO (82-1): student
60-7　　10	ノ ク イ 彳 彳 彳 往 往 徎 徒

恰	* 恰好 KAKKŌ (82-6): allure, appearance
61-6 *　　9	丶 丶 忄 忄 忄 忄 恰 恰 恰

浅	*asa(i)*: to be shallow 浅草 *asakusa* (82-8): Asakusa
85-6　　9	丶 丶 氵 浐 浅 浅 浅

草	*kusa* (82-8), SŌ (83-2): grass, herbs 雑草 ZASSŌ: weeds
140-6　　9	一 艹 艹 苩 草 苩 草

偽	*nise* (82-10), GI: imitation, lie, false 偽証 GISHŌ: perjury, false testimony
9-9　　11	ノ イ イ 伫 伊 伊 偽 偽

宝	*takara*, HŌ (82-10): treasure, jewelry 宝石 HŌSEKI (82-10): gems, precious stones
40-5　　8	⺌　⺍　宀　宀　宀　宇　宝　宝
宅	TAKU (82-11): house, residence お宅 *o*TAKU (82-11): your house (high degree)
40-3　　6	⺌　⺍　宀　宀　宀　宅
若	*waka(i)* (83-1): to be young
140-5　　8	一　十　艹　艹　芒　芒　若　若
懸	KEN (83-2): to hang up 一生懸命 ISSHŌKENMEI (83-2): with all one's might
61-16　　20	目　且　県　県　県　県　県　懸　懸
源	*minamoto*, GEN (83-2): source 源氏物語 GENJI*monogatari* (83-2): *The Tale of Genji*
85-10 13	⺀　ミ　シ　汀　沪　沪　沪　沪　源　源　源

氏	SHI (83-2): clan, family; Mr. 氏族 SHIZOKU: clan
83-0 4	´ ㇄ ㇇ 氏
典	TEN (83-2): code, rite 辞典 JITEN: dictionary
12-6 8	丨 冂 冂 冉 冊 曲 典 典
漫	MAN (83-2): involuntary 漫画 MANGA (83-2): comics, cartoon, Manga
85-11 14	氵 氵 沪 沪 渭 渭 漫 漫
図	TO (83-3), <u>ZU</u>: plan, map, schema 図書館 TOSHOKAN (83-3): library 図案 ZUAN: drawing
31-4 7	丨 冂 冂 冈 図 図 図
清	*kiyo(i)*, SEI (83-5): to be pure, to be clear 清掃 SEISŌ: cleaning up
85-8 11	氵 氵 氵 汁 洼 清 清 清 清

納	NŌ, NA (83-5): to fulfill (obligations), to carry to term
	納付 NŌFU: to pay (taxes) 納得 NATTOKU: acquiescence, agreement
120-4　　10	く　纟　纟　纟　糸　糸　糽　紈　納　納

暗	kura(i), AN (83-5): to be dark
	暗記 ANKI (83-5): learning by heart, memory work
72-9　　13	丨　冂　日　日　日'　旷　旷　旷　晬　暗　暗

紫	murasaki (83-6): purple
120-6　　12	丨　丨　止　止　止'　此　此　紫　紫

流	naga(reru), RYŪ (83-6): to flow
	女流作家 JORYŪSAKKA (83-6): female author 流行 RYŪKŌ: popular, fashion
85-7　　10	冫　冫　氵　汽　汽　沪　泸　泸　流　流

廷	TEI (83-7): imperial court
	朝廷 CHŌTEI (83-7): Imperial Court
54-4　　7	ノ　二　千　壬　廷　廷

魔	MA (83-9): evil spirit, demon 邪魔 JAMA (83-9): obstacle, obstruction, disturbance
194-11 21	亠 广 庂 庥 庨 麿 麿 麿 魔 魔

閣	KAKU (85-title): tour; cabinet (in government) 内閣 NAIKAKU: ministry, government cabinet
169-6 14	丨 冂 冂 閂 閁 門 門 門 閉 閣 閣

池	*ike* (85-2): basin, pool, pond
85-3 6	丶 冫 氵 沪 汕 池

復	FUKU (85-4): to return to, to come back to 復元 FUKUGEN (85-4): restoration, reconstruction 復習 FUKUSHŪ (99-7): revisions
60-9 12	彳 彳 彳 犷 彳 犷 復 復 復 復

完	KAN (85-5): totality, whole 完全 KANZEN: complete, perfect
40-4 7	丶 宀 宀 宀 宇 完

璧	HEKI, -PEKI (85-5): jewel
	完璧 KANPEKI (85-5): impeccable, perfect, without fault
96-13* 18	⁻ 尸 吕 启 启⁻ 辟⁻ 辟 辟 璧 璧
求	*moto(meru)* (85-5), KYŪ: to ask, to search for
	求職 KYŪSHOKU: job application
85-2 7	一 十 寸 才 求 求 求
耐	*ta(eru)* (85-5): to endure, to bear
126-3 9	一 ⁻ 厂 丙 而 而 耐 耐
燃	*mo(eru)* (86-12), NEN: to burn
	燃料 NENRYŌ: fuel
86-12 16	′ 火 火 灯 灼 炒 燃 燃 燃
嘘	*uso* (85-7): lie, falsehood
30-12* 15	口 口′ 口ᵇ 吓 吁 吁 唭 唭 嘘 嘘

造	ZŌ (85-7): construction 木造 MOKUZŌ (85-7): wood construction
162-7 10	ノ 广 牛 生 告 告 告 告 造 造
紀	KI (85-8): annals, history, recording 紀元前 KIGENZEN: B.C. 紀元後 KIGENGO: A.D.
120-3 9	く 幺 幺 爷 糸 紀 紀 紀
霧	FUN (85-9): fog, mist 霧囲気 FUN.IKI (85-9): atmosphere, ambiance
173-4 12	一 广 广 币 雨 雫 雫 雫 雺 霧
囲	*kako(mu)*, I (85-9): to enclose, to surround 周囲 SHŪI: circumference, periphery
31-4 7	l 冂 冂 冃 囝 囲 囲
際	SAI (85-9): moment, occasion 実際 JISSAI (85-9): truth, reality 国際 KOKUSAI (92-ex. 5): international
170-11 14	㇇ ㇖ 阝 阝 阝 阝 阝 阽 阽 陉 際

印	IN (85-10): mark, stamp 印刷 INSATSU: imprint
26-4　　6	´ ´ ´ ´ 印 印

吉	*yoshi* (86-3), KICHI (88-9): luck, good fortune
30-3　　6	一 十 士 吉 吉 吉

慮	RYO (86-7): consideration, thought 遠慮 ENRYO (86-7): discretion, reserve
61-11　　15	` ⺊ ⼴ 广 庐 虍 虎 唐 膚 膚 慮

嫁	*yome* (86-10): young woman, step-daughter *嫁先 totsugisaki (86-8): family into which a woman marries
38-10　　13	く 夕 女 妒 妒 妒 婷 嫁 嫁 嫁

突	TOTSU (86-14): to pierce, to attack, to hit 突然 TOTSUZEN (86-14): suddenly
116-3　　8	` ` 宀 宀 突 空 突 突

訪	*tazu(neru)* (86-14), HŌ: to visit 訪問 HŌMON: visit
149-4　11	、 ユ ゴ 言 言 言 言 言' 訪 訪 訪
訳	*wake* (86-14): reason, signification; <u>YAKU</u> (95-1): translation 通訳 TSŪYAKU (97-11): interpreter
149-4　11	言 言' 言' 訳 訳 訳

筈	*hazu* (87-3): what will be or should be
118-6　12	ノ ヶ ヶ 竹 竹 竹 竿 竿 筈
状	JŌ (87-8): circumstances 状態 JŌTAI (87-8): current state, conditions, circumstance
94-3　7	㇀ ㇀ ㇀ ㇀ ㇀ ㇀ 状 状
態	TAI (87-7): appearance 態度 TAIDO: attitude
61-10　14	⺦ ㄙ 台 台 台 能 能 態 態

貨	KA (88-title): merchandise, freight 貨物 KAMOTSU: merchandise, freight
154-4　　11	ノ イ イ 亻ヒ 化 化 伫 眥 眥 貨 貨

幣	HEI (88-title): folded paper offered in Shinto ceremonies 貨幣 KAHEI (88-title): money
50-12　　15	ノ ソ 尚 尚 米 紫 紫 敝 敝 幣 幣

破	*yabu(ru)* (88-3): to destroy, to break
112-5　　10	一 厂 丆 石 石 矿 矿 砂 破 破

描	*ega(ku)* (88-4), BYŌ: to paint, to draw, to describe 描写 BYŌSHA: description, painting
64-8　　11	一 十 扌 扩 打 描 描 描 描

聖	SEI, *SHŌ* (88-5): saint, sage; sainthood 聖人 SEIJIN: a saint
128-7　　13	一 厂 F 耳 耴 耶 即 聖 聖

徳	TOKU (88-5): virtue; gain 道徳 DŌTOKU: morality, ethics
60-11　　14	ク イ 彳 彳 彳 徉 徏 徔 徳 徳
憲	KEN (88-5): law 憲法 KENPŌ (88-5): the Constitution
61-12　　16	` ⺍ 宀 宁 宇 宔 害 寓 寓 憲
視	SHI (88-7): to consider, to look at 視覚 SHIKAKU: sight, visual perception
147-4　　11	` ラ ネ ネ 初 祀 祖 祖 視
福	FUKU (88-9): luck, good fortune 幸福 KŌFUKU: fortune
113-9　　13	` ラ ネ ネ ネ 祠 祠 福 福 福
諭	YU (88-9): to advise, to light 説諭 SETSUYU: reproof
149-9　　16	` 言 言 訃 訡 諭 諭 諭 諭

維	I (88-10): cord, link 維新 ISHIN (88-10): the Meiji Restoration
120-8　　14	く 幺 幺 幺 糸 糸 糸 糸 紵 紵 維

欧	Ō (88-10): Europe 欧米 ŌBEI (88-10): the West, Europe and America
76-4　　8	一 ７ 又 区 区 欧 欧 欧

米	*kome*, BEI: rice; BEI (88-10): the USA, American 米国 BEIKOKU: America, the USA
119-0　　6	丶 丷 二 半 米

稲	*ine, ina-* (88-11): rice stalks
115-9　　14	′ 二 千 禾 禾 秆 秆 稲 稲

昭	SHŌ (88-11): brilliant, bright 昭和 SHŌWA (88-11): the Shōwa Era (1926-1989)
72-5　　9	丨 冂 日 日 日７ 日刀 日刀 昭 昭

| 育 | *soda(teru)*, IKU (88-11): to raise, to educate

教育 KYŌIKU (92-11): education, instruction |
| 130-4　8 | ` 一 亠 云 云 产 产 育 育 |

| 輩 | HAI (88-13), -PAI: companion

先輩 SENPAI: elders, the ancient |
| 159-8　15 | ノ ヲ 扎 非 非 非 輩 輩 輩 輩 |

| 勧 | *susu(meru)* (88-15), KAN: to recommend, to advise

勧告 KANKOKU: recommendation, advice |
| 19-11　13 | ノ ヒ ヒ ケ ケ 午 年 佯 雀 雀 勧 勧 |

| 桜 | *sakura* (89-1): cherry tree |
| 75-6　10 | 一 十 才 木 杉 杉 杉 桜 桜 桜 |

| 諺 | *kotowaza* (89-3): proverb, maxim |
| 149-9　16 | 言 言 言 言 言 診 諺 諺 諺 |

善	<u>ZEN</u> (89-5): the good, the right, virtue 善意 ZEN.I: good will, good intentions
30-9　　12	丷　半　兰　半　羊　羊　美　善　善
信	SHIN (89-8): fidelity, sincerity 信用 SHIN.YŌ: credit, trust
9-7　　9	ノ　イ　イ　仁　仁　仨　信　信　信
墨	*sumi* (89-9): ink, India ink
32-11　　14	ノ　冂　日　甲　甲　里　黒　黒　墨　墨
短	*mijika(i)* (97-ex. 1), TAN (89-9): to be short 短歌 TANKA (89-9): short poem, tanka (poetic form)
111-7　　12	ノ　ヒ　午　矢　矢　知　知　短　短
詠	*yo(mu)* (89-9): to compose poetry
149-5　　12	丶　言　言　言　言　訂　訟　詠　詠

| 笑 | *wara(u)* (89-13): to laugh |
| 118-4　　10 | ノ ⺮ ⺮ ⺮ ⺮ ⺮ 笑 笑 笑 笑 |

| 吸 | *su(u)* (89-ex. 3), KYŪ: to breathe, to inhale, to suck

呼吸 KOKYŪ: breath |
| 30-3　　6 | ⼁ ⼝ ⼝ ⼝ 吸 吸 |

| 波 | *nami* (89-ex. 4): waves |
| 85-5　　8 | ⼂ ⼓ ⼓ ⼓ 沪 沪 波 波 |

| 就 | SHŪ (90-2): to take (a place)

就職 SHŪSHOKU: the act of finding a job |
| 43-9　　12 | ⼂ ⼟ 古 亨 京 京 莿 就 就 |

| 費 | HI (90-2): cost, fee

学費 GAKUHI (90-2): tuition |
| 154-5　　12 | ⼸ ⼸ 弓 弗 弗 弗 弗 弗 費 |

身	*mi* (90-5), SHIN: body, person 身分 *mi*BUN: identity, social status 自身 JISHIN: oneself
158-0　　7	´ ｒ ｒ 冃 刯 身 身

授	JU (90-6): to give, to confer 教授 KYŌJU (90-6): teaching, professor
64-8　　11	一 十 才 扌 扩 扩 护 护 抐 授

頼	*tano(mu)* (90-6), RAI: to ask, to pray 信頼 SHINRAI: trust, faith
154-9　　16	一 ロ 市 束 柬 柬 頼 頼 頼 頼

放	*hana(su)*, HŌ (92-4): to leave alone, to free 放映 HŌEI (92-5): broadcast (a movie) on television
66-4　　8	` 二 亓 方 方 放 放 放

種	SHU (92-4): variety, sort, kind 種類 SHURUI (92-4): sort
115-9　　14	ノ 二 千 禾 禾 秆 秆 秤 稆 種 種

豊	*yuta(ka)*, HŌ (92-4): rich, fertile 豊富 HŌFU (92-4): abundant, copious
151-6　　13	丶 冂 冎 曲 曲 豊 豊 豊 豊
劇	GEKI (92-5): a play, theatre 現代劇 GENDAIGEKI (92-5): modern theatre
18-13　　15	丨 𠂆 广 庐 庐 虍 虏 虜 豦 劇
娯	GO (92-8): pleasure, amusement 娯楽 GORAKU (92-8): pastime, distraction, diversion
38-7　　10	𡿨 夂 女 好 妒 妒 妒 娯 娯
縫	*nu(u)*, HŌ (92-9): to sew, to embroider 裁縫 SAIHŌ (92-9): sewing
120-10　　16	𡿨 幺 糸 糹 終 終 縫 縫 縫
琴	*koto* (92-9): the koto, the zither
96-8　　12	一 丁 王 王 珡 珡 珡 琴 琴

講	KŌ (92-9): association; conference 講座 KŌZA (92-9): a lecture course
149-10　　17	言 言 言 言 計 講 講 講 講 講 講

企	KI (92-13): plan, design 企業 KIGYŌ (92-13): enterprise, company
9-4　　　6	ノ 人 个 仐 企 企

告	KOKU (92-14): to inform, to announce 予告 YOKOKU: advance notice, warning, advance billing
30-4　　　7	ノ ⺊ 十 牛 牛 告 告

殊	SHU (92-ex. 3): special, exceptional 特殊 TOKUSHU (92-ex. 3): particular, special
78-6　　10	一 ヌ 歹 歹 歹 殀 殊 殊

弁	BEN (93-1): discrimination; discourse お弁当 oBENTŌ (93-1): take-away meal
55-2　　　5	⼂ ム ⼛ 弁 弁

| 鳥 | *tori* (93-2): bird |
| 196-0　11 | ´ ㇇ ㇒ 户 阜 鳥 鳥 鳥 |

| 煮 | *ni(ru)* (93-2): to bring to a boil

お煮染 *onishime* (93-2): a kind of stew |
| 86-8　12 | 一 十 土 耂 耂 者 者 煮 |

| 染 | *so(meru)*: to dye, to color; *shi(miru)* (93-2): to infiltrate, to impregnate

染物屋 *somemonoya*: dye salon, dyehouse |
| 75-5　9 | ` ㇀ 氵 氿 沈 沈 染 染 |

| 努 | *tsuto(meru)* (93-2), DO: effort, diligence

努力 DORYOKU: effort |
| 19-5　7 | ㇈ 女 女 奴 奴 努 努 |

| 茹 | *yu(deru)*, *u(deru)* (93-2): to bring to a boil

茹卵 *yudetamago* (93-2): hard-boiled eggs |
| 140-6*　9 | 一 艹 艹 艾 芗 芴 茹 茹 |

報	HŌ (93-3): news; reward 天気予報 TENKIYOHŌ (93-3): weather forecast 報告 HŌKOKU: report
32-9　　12	十　土　圥　坴　幸　幸￢　報ﾞ　報　報
曇	kumo(ru): to be cloudy; kumo(ri) (93-3): cloudy weather
72-12　　16	冖　曰　目　咼　杲　杲　杲　曇　曇
晴	hareru (93-3): to be clear (sky)
72-8　　12	丨　冂　日　日￢　日￢　日十　晴　晴　晴　晴
重	omo(i) (93-5), JŪ: to be heavy, to be serious 重要 JŪYŌ: important
166-2　　9	丿　一　亼　后　盲　盲　重　重　重
腹	hara, (o)naka (93-6): abdomen, stomach
130-9　　13	刀　月　月　肐　肐　胩　腜　腹　腹

甘		*ama(i)* (93-9): to be sweet, to be soft
99-0	5	一 十 廿 甘 甘

困		*koma(ru)* (93-ex. 4): to be embarrassed, to be annoyed
31-4	7	丨 冂 冂 円 用 闲 困 困

賓		HIN (94-2): guest 賓客 HINKYAKU: guest of honor
154-8	15	宀 宀 宀 宋 宇 宁 宕 宕 賓

込		*ko(mu)*: to be cluttered; *ko(mi)*, *-go(mi)* (94-2): mixture 人込み *hitogomi* (94-2): a crowd of people
162-2	5	ノ 入 込 込 込

警		KEI (94-3): to make reprimands, to reproach 警察 KEISATSU (94-3): the police
149-12	19	艹 广 芍 苟 苟 敬 敬 警 警

察	SATSU (94-3): to suppose, to understand
	考察 KŌSATSU: observation, reflection
40-11 14	宀 宀 宀 宀 宀 宊 突 寮 寮 察

官	KAN (94-3): the authorities, government
	官僚 KANRYŌ: functionary, bureaucrat
40-5 8	' ハ 宀 宀 宁 官 官 官

総	SŌ (94-3): entire, total
	総合 SŌGŌ: synthesis
120-8 14	く 幺 糸 糸 糸 紗 紗 紛 総 総

臣	SHIN, JIN (94-3): subject, vassal
	総理大臣 SŌRIDAIJIN (94-3): Prime Minister
131-0 7	l 厂 厂 厂 臣 臣 臣 臣

王	Ō (94-3): king
	女王 JOŌ (94-3): queen
96-0 4	一 T 干 王

席	SEKI (94-6): seat, place
	予約席 YOYAKUSEKI: reserved seats
50-7　　10	' 亠 广 广 庐 庐 庶 庶 席

系	KEI (94-11): system, lineage
	理科系 RIKAKEI (94-11): the sciences
120-1　　7	ノ 丆 互 玄 系 系 系

号	GŌ (95-title): number; name
	年号 NENGŌ (95-title): name of an era
30-2　　5	' 口 口 므 号

抄	SHŌ (95-1): choice, selection; copy
	戸籍抄本 KOSEKISHŌHON (95-1): abstract of one's family register
64-4　　7	一 十 扌 扚 扚 抄 抄

暦	*koyomi*, REKI (95-1): calendar
	西暦 SEIREKI (95-1): the Western calendar
72-10　　14	一 厂 厈 厈 厈 厤 厤 暦 暦

注	CHŪ (95-1): note, commentary 注意 CHŪI: attention 注意書き CHŪ*gaki* (95-1): notes, annotations
85-5　　8	`丶　丶　氵　氵　汀　汗　汼　注`

引	*hi(ku)* (95-ex. 2): to pull off, to take away
57-1　　4	`フ　コ　弓　引`

割	*wa(ru)* (95-ex. 4): to divide 割り引き *waribiki*: reduction, rebate
18-10　　12	`丶　宀　宀　中　宔　宝　害　割　割`

存	SON, ZON (96-2): to know, to feel 御存知 GOZONJI (96-2): to know (high degree, you)
39-3　　6	`一　ナ　才　存　存　存`

弾	*hi(ku)* (96-10): to play an instrument; DAN: bullet, bomb 弾薬 DAN.YAKU: ammunition
57-9　　12	`フ　コ　弓　弓゛　弓゛　弴゛　弾　弾　弾`

捕	*tsukama(eru)* (96-ex. 2), *tora(eru)*: to capture, to arrest
64-7　　10	一 十 扌 扌 扩 折 折 捐 捕 捕
弟	*otōto* (96-ex. 4): younger brother *弟子 DESHI: student, disciple
57-4　　7	丶 丷 丷 긋 肖 弟 弟

巡	JUN: to turn around, tour about 巡回 JUNKAI: rounds, patrol *お巡りさん *omawarisan* (97-1): police officer
47-3　　6	く 巛 巛 ツ 巡 巡
牛	*ushi* (97-7), GYŪ: cow, bull 牛肉 GYŪNIKU: beef
93-0　　4	ノ ヒ ニ 牛
姓	SEI, SHŌ (97-7): family name 百姓 HYAKUSHŌ: common people
38-5　　8	く 女 女 女 女 姓 姓 姓

修	*osa(maru)*, SHŪ (97-9): to control oneself, to get a grip on oneself; *osa(meru)*, SHŪ (97-9): to study, to master 修学旅行 SHŪGAKURYOKŌ (97-9): school excursion
9-8　　　　10	ノ 亻 亻 亻 亻 亻 修 修

築	CHIKU (97-9): to construct 建築家 KENCHIKUKA (97-9): architect
118-10　　16	ノ ケ ケケ ケケ ケケ ケケ ケケ 筑 筑 築

形	*katachi* (97-9), KEI: form; model 形式 KEISHIKI: form, formality
59-4　　　　7	一 二 干 开 开 形 形

遂	*tsui(ni)* (97-11): finally; SUI: to accomplish 遂行 SUIKŌ: accomplishment, performance
162-9　　12	丷 艹 丷 芋 芋 芧 豕 㒸 遂 遂

俳	HAI (97-11): actor 俳句 HAIKU: haiku, 17-syllable form poem
9-8　　　　10	ノ 亻 亻 付 付 侟 侟 俳 俳

則	SOKU (99-7): to be based on, to be modeled on; law, rule 規則 KISOKU (99-7): rule, regulation
18-7　　　9	丨　冂　冃　月　目　貝　貝　貝　則　則
冊	SATSU (99-7): *measure word for books* 二冊 NISATSU: two (books) 二冊目 NISATSU*me* (99-7): the second book
13-3　　　5	丨　冂　冂　冊　冊
得	TOKU (99-11): profit, benefit 所得 SHOTOKU: income
60-8　　　11	′　彳　彳　彳　彳　得　得　得　得　得
里	RI (99-12): a league (4 km; 3 miles) 千里 SENRI (99-12): a thousand leagues
166-0　　　7	丶　冂　日　日　甲　里　里
伴	HAN (99-15): to accompany 伴侶 HANRYO (99-15): companion
9-5　　　7	ノ　亻　亻　亻　亻　亻　伴

	RYO (99-15): companion
侶	好伴侶 KŌHANRYO (99-15): faithful companion
9-7 9	ノ 亻 亻 亻 亻 侶 侶 侶 侶 侶

APPENDIXES

APPENDIX 1

The Radicals

The 214 radicals of this table represent the traditional classification system invented in China and still in use today.

The radicals themselves are organized based on the number of strokes, from 1 to 17. The number is indicated by the large digits in the table below, preceding the listed radicals.

We have presented the radicals, as is common with dictionaries, with each radical in a separate box. In each box, we have included:

• the **number** of the radical (you may want to remember these numbers, at least for the most common radicals. You'll save yourself lots of time with Japanese dictionaries in the future if you don't have to hunt for the radical each time you look up a character!)

• the **radical** itself. Many radicals have more than one form, depending on whether it is written independently, or as part of a character, and where in the character (top, bottom, left, right) the radical appears. We have often included the different forms of the same radical (cf. for instance radicals 9, 12, 42…)

• the **meaning** of the radical.

	1	**1** — one	**2** 丨 line
3 丶 dot	**4** 丿	**5** 乙 second	**6** 亅 hook

	7 二 two	8 土 press	9 人 亻 八 person
2			
10 儿 legs	11 入 enter	12 八 八 eight	13 冂 edge
14 ⼍ lid	15 冫 ice	16 几 table	17 凵 open box
18 刀 knife	19 力 power	20 勹 package	21 匕 ladle
22 匚 box	23 匸 chest	24 十 ten	25 卜 divination
26 卩 㔾 measure	27 厂 cliff	28 厶 me	29 又 again
3	30 口 mouth	31 囗 enclosure	32 土 earth
33 士 servant	34 夂 winter	35 夊	36 夕 evening

212

37 大 big	38 女 woman	39 子 child	40 宀 roof
41 寸 inch	42 小丷 small	43 尢 twisted legs	44 尸 corpse
45 屮 sprout	46 山 mountain	47 川巛 river	48 工 worker
49 己巳 self	50 巾 tissue	51 干 dry	52 幺 very thin
53 广 shelter	54 夂 to go	55 廾 offering	56 弋 javelin
57 弓 bow	58 互彐彑 snout	59 彡 brush tip	60 彳 step
4	61 心忄 小 heart	62 戈 battle-axe	63 戶 door
64 手扌 hand	65 支 branch	66 支攵 strike	67 文 letters

213

68	69	70	71
斗	斤	方	无旡
bushel	hatchet	direction	without
72	**73**	**74**	**75**
日	曰	月	木
sun	talk	moon	wood
76	**77**	**78**	**79**
欠	止	歹	殳
lease	stop	death	lance
80	**81**	**82**	**83**
母毋	比	毛	氏
mother	compare	fur	clan
84	**85**	**86**	**87**
气	水氵	火灬	爪爫
vapor	water	fire	claws
88	**89**	**90**	**91**
父	爻	丬	片
father	mixture	platform	side
92	**93**	**94**	
牙	牛	犬犭	**5**
tooth	cow	dog	
95	**96**	**97**	**98**
玄	玉王	瓜	瓦
mysterious	jade	melon	tile

99 甘 sweet	100 生 life	101 用 use	102 田 rice field
103 𤴓 正 legs	104 疒 sickness	105 癶 footsteps	106 白 white
107 皮 skin	108 皿 plate	109 目 eye	110 矛 spear
111 矢 arrow	112 石 stone	113 示 ネ display,rituals	114 禸 imprint
115 禾 tuft	116 穴 cavity	117 立 stand	**6**
118 竹 bamboo	119 米 rice	120 糸 silk	121 缶 jar
122 网 冈 罒 罘 web	123 羊 羋 sheep	124 羽 feathers	125 老 耂 old
126 而 but	127 耒 plow	128 耳 ear	129 聿 brush

130 肉月 flesh	131 臣 vassal	132 自 self	133 至 attain
134 臼 mortar	135 舌 tongue	136 舛 turn away	137 舟 boat
138 艮 disagreement	139 色 color	140 艹 grass	141 虍 tiger
142 虫 worm, insect	143 血 blood	144 行 go	145 衣衤 clothes
146 両西 cover	7	147 見 see	148 角 horn
149 言 speech	150 谷 valley	151 豆 bean	152 豕 hog
153 豸 animal	154 貝 shell	155 赤 crimson	156 走 run
157 足 foot	158 身 body	159 車 car	160 辛 strong, spicy

161 辰 dragon (zodiac)	162 辶 walking	163 阝 hamlet	164 酉 wine jar
165 釆 sow	166 里 village	8	167 金 metal
168 長 long	169 門 gates	170 阝 hill	171 隶 purchase
172 隹 short-tailed bird	173 雨 rain	174 青 blue-green	175 非 *negative*
9	176 面 face	177 革 leather	178 韋 tanned skin
179 韭 garlic	180 音 sound	181 頁 head	182 風 wind
183 飛 flight	184 食 eat	185 首 head, neck	186 香 fragrance
10	187 馬 horse	188 骨 bone	189 高 height

190 髟 hair	191 鬥 battle	192 鬯 fragrant herb	193 鬲 tripod
194 鬼 ghost	11	195 魚 fish	196 鳥 long-tailed bird
197 鹵 salt	198 鹿 deer	199 麥麦 wheat	200 麻 hemp
12	201 黃 yellow	202 黍 millet	203 黑 black
204 黹 sew	13	205 黽 frog	206 鼎 metal tripod
207 鼓 drum	208 鼠 mouse	14	209 鼻 nose
210 齊 purification	15	211 齒 tooth	16
212 龍 dragon	213 龜 turtle	17	214 龠 flute

218

APPENDIX 2

Texts of Lessons from Volumes 1 & 2
of *Japanese with Ease*

For the presentation of these texts, we have used the normal page-layout for written Japanese; that is, we've put the text in vertical columns.

Vertical Japanese text is read from right to left. Thus, a Japanese book is written exactly opposite from ours: the first page is on the right, and the cover of books is where we find the backsides of ours.

These following texts constitute a "mini-book" within this volume (just to whet your appetite!), running from page 259 to 220!

の日本語は片足で歩こうとするようなもの
です。大丈夫ですよ、三冊目の漢字の本を
一緒に勉強しましょう。ゆっくりと、無理
なく、しかし完璧に。外国語を会得するの
は、何語であっても、時間がかかります。
一番大切な事は、まず、始めることです。
日本に大変面白い諺があります。「千里の行
も一歩より始まる」。一歩一歩、かなり進み
ましたね。次に大切な事は続けることです。
そのためにはこれらのアシミルの本はあな
たの好伴侶にならなくてはなりません。何
度でも、レッスンを勉強しなおして下さい。
問題も書き取りもやりなおして下さい。話
す機会を自分からどんどん作って下さい。
あなたならできますよ。ではがんばって、
続けて下さい。さようなら。

220

のように、学校が終わると、近所の工場へ行って、トラックが出たり入ったりするのを見ていました。」「その次は何になりたくなったの。」「北海道の伯父さんは広い農場を持っています。六年生の夏休みは伯父さんのところで過ごしました。トラクターを運転したり、牛の世話をしたりして過ごしました。将来はお百姓さんになりたいと思いました。」「それからどうしたの。」「中学生の時、修学旅行で東京まで来て、オリンピックのために建てたスタジアムなどを見、建築家とは夢を形に表すことのできる職業だと思いました。」「それからどうなったのですか。」「高校を卒業するころは、外国旅行がしたかったなろうかと思いましたが、遂に、商社マンか通訳に、一回でも子供の時からりました。そうすれば、これらの職業にみんなつからと夢に見ていた

くことができるからです。」

第九十九課　最後に　よく日本語はむずかしいと言われていますが、あなたは正直言って、どう思いますか。アシミルのおかげで日本語を「無理なく」覚えたでしょう。ご存は話すことも、平仮名と片仮名を読むことも書くこともできるでしょう。それに面白いでしょうね！すばらしいでしょう。それだけでなく、日本についてもその上、言葉だけでなく、日本についていろいろな事がわかるようになったでしょう。いろいろですから今ここでやめてはいけません。まだ、勉強する事がたくさんありますから今この二冊目のレッスンを一つずつやりなおすのです。カセットを聞いて、テキストを暗記するくらい勉強して下さい。ところで、だ漢字が残っていますね。でももうどれが漢字ぬきどの字か見ればわかるでしょう。

221

明治元年は確か一八六八年だから、それに三十年を足すと一八九八年だわ。」「お祖父さんのお父さんは、十九世紀に生まれたのか。すごいな。」

第九十六課　ピアノを買う

「娘がピアノを習いたいと言うので、習わせようと思っています。どなたかいい先生を御存知だったら、紹介して下さいませんか。レッスンを始める前に、ピアノを買おうと思いますが、あなたはピアノにくわしいから一緒に見ていただけますか。」店で「こんなにピアノの種類があるとは知りませんでした。」「グランド・ピアノですか。アップライト・ピアノですか。」「これから始めるのだからアップライト・ピアノにしましょう。」「どのメーカーになさいますか。外国製または国産のもございます。色は黒いのも白いのも茶色のもございます。どれになさいますか。」

「ピアノは外観ではなく、音で決めるものよ。弾いてみないとわからないわよ。こちらのは深みがある音ね。あちらのは私の好きな音ではないわ。そちらのはどうかしら。」「どれにしたらいいのかわからないわ。決められないから、今日はカタログだけいただいて帰ります。じゃあ今日はやめておきます。」

第九十七課　職業

「小学校の一年生の時、母とショッピング・センターへ買物に行って、迷子になりました。その時あまりにもこわくてどうなるかと思っていたら、親切なお巡りさんが交番へ連れていってくれて、そのことから家まで送ってくれました。そのことがあまりにもうれしかったので、将来はお巡りさんになりたいと思いました。」「それから、トラックの運転手になりたかったので、毎日

込みで、車が全然通れませんでした。車の
そばにいた警察官に『どなたがいらしたの
ですか』と聞いてみたら、『総理大臣がオラ
ンダの女王を御案内しているところです』
と言われました。迎賓館を出て、国会議事
堂の方へ向かうところなのだそうです。と
ころで今月の父兄会にいらっしゃいます
か。」「出席するつもりです。今度の国語の
先生をどうお思いになりますか。」「娘の話
によると、明るい感じの方だそうですが、
とてもきびしい点をお付けになるみたいで
す。」「内の娘は新しい理科の先生のことを
よく話します。やさしくて、その上、美男
子なので、娘はすっかり先生のファンにな
ってしまいました。今年になってから、今
まできらいだった理科が急に好きになって、
将来は理科系の仕事がしたいと言っていま
す。去年までは、国語の先生がよかったの
で、新聞記者になると言っていました。こ
の調子だと、来年は何か他のものになりた
がるでしょう。」

第九十五課　年号

「戸籍抄本を訳しても
らうために大使館へ行ったのだけれど、『年
号は西暦で書かなければいけない』と注意
書きがあるんだ。めんどうくさいよ。」「え
え、大正十三年は何年になるかな」「ちょ
っと待って下さい。一九一二年は大正元年
に当たるから、大正十三年は、一九一二年
に十二年足せばいいんじゃない？一九二四
年になるわけ。」「おれたちが結婚したのは昭
和二十三年。」「昭和元年は何年だったかな。」
「一九二六年です。」「じゃあ一九二六年に
二十二を足すと一九四八年になるなあ。」
「一九二六年を取ったわけだなあ。」「お祖父さ
んのお父さんは確か明治生まれだよね。明
治何年の生まれだったかしら。」「明治三十一
年だよ。」「ということは、西

れ？」

育テレビで放送されている。でも僕が一番好きな番組は、ホーム・ドラマで、それを見ていると、日本の家族の人間関係のことがよくわかる。民間放送の場合は一つ一つの番組が、いくつかの企業のスポンサーによって放送される。だから放送中にその企業の広告がよくある。最初は物語が途中で中断されるのでいらいらしたが、このごろはその時を利用して、お茶のためにお湯を沸かしたり、トイレに立ったりできるので、便利だと思う。もうじき僕の好きな時代劇が始まるので、今日はこれぐらいにします。お元気で。

第九十三課　遠足　「明日の遠足、うれしいな。お母さん、お弁当に何を作ってくれるの。」「今晩のおかずは鳥と野菜のお煮染だったから、それを少し取っておいてあげましたよ。それに努が大好きな茹卵二つ。」

「天気予報だと、午前中は曇りだけど、午後は晴れるそうだから、よかったな。」「先生が明日はたくさん歩くとおっしゃっていましたから、お結びは五つ入れますよ。」「お結び、五つ？そんなに食べられないよ。」「でもリュック・サックも重くなるから嫌だよ。」「でもお腹がすいていたら、歩けませんよ。」「デザートとお八つには何を準備してくれたの。」「りんごとお煎餅よ。」「それだけ？甘いものは何もないの。チョコレートとクッキーがほしいなあ。」「あら、だって、努がさっき言ったでしょう？……リュック・サックが重くなるって……さあ……あまり遅くならないうちに、寝なさい。」「うん……お母さん、お休みなさい。」

第九十四課　日常会話　「遅れてしまって申しわけありません。タクシーに乗ったのですが、迎賓館の前を通った時、すごい人

安いですから。」「その為には高校から東京にやらなくちゃね。姉さんの所で預かってもらえばいいよ。」「中学校の一年生から英語をしっかりと身につけさせましょう。お隣の大学生は英語が達者だと聞きましたから、個人教授をしてくれるように頼みましょう。これからの社会は国際的になってしょう。これからの社会は国際的になっていくから、なんといっても、語学がものをいいますからね。」「でも中学校に入るまでいいですから。」「そうすると、小学校もよほどできなければだめだな。」「場合によっては、小学校だけでも私立にしてもいいわを選ばなければなりません。」「そうなると幼稚園も問題だね。」「そうなると東京の姉さんに電話したらどうだ?さっそく東ろで『善は急げ』と言うから、あなた達はちょっとせっかち過ぎるのじゃない?和生は生まれてまだ九日でしょう。そんな先のことはもっと後でいいのじゃない?」

第九十二課　日本のテレビ　ベルナール

君、その後、元気かい。君が僕と一緒に日本へこられなかったのはとても残念だ。テレビの好きな君はきっと日本のテレビが気に入るだろうと思う。日本には公共放送のNHKが二チャンネルある他、民間放送がたくさんあるので、番組の種類はとても豊富だ。映画は欧米のものも随分放映されているし、日本のものは現代劇も時代劇もあるよ。クイズや漫画の番組も盛んだよ。日本のテレビには何でもあって、お見合い番組もあるんだ。でも日本のテレビは娯楽のための番組だけではなく、勉強のための番組もあるまでである。それは料理、裁縫から始まってバイオリン、ピアノ、フルート、ギター、琴、三味線などの楽器や外国語の講座もある。その他大学の数学、社会学などの講座も聞くことができる。それはほとんどNHKの教

225

であり、農業の研究を色々した人です。千円札は夏目漱石という日本の近代文学の有名な作家です。特に知られている作品は『吾輩は猫である』という小説で、一九〇五年に書かれた作品です。猫が主人公で、猫の目で見た人間の社会が描かれています。とても面白いですから、まだ読んでいないのでしたら、ぜひお読みになるようお勧めします。」

第八十九課　花見　「皇居のそばにある桜の木は満開になりましたね。」「きっと上野公園の桜も二日三日の内に満開になるでしょう。」「そうですね。桜の花は散るのが速いですからね。『三日見ぬ間の桜かな』と言う諺があるくらいですからね。」「去年も一昨年も出張していたので、桜の花をゆっくりと見る暇がありませんでしたが、今年はそうですぜひ行きたいと思っています。」

ね。『善は急げ』と言いますから、明日の午後にでもいかがですか。」「桜の花を見ている と、子供の頃のことを思い出します。」「お国はどちらでしたっけね。」「信州です。」「信州の毎年四月になると私の祖父は庭にある大きな桜の木の下に莫蓙を敷き、午後中、そこに座って、お酒を飲みながら花を見ていました。時々墨などを持ってこさせ、短歌などを詠んでいました。私は姉と一緒によく祖父の莫蓙の上でままごとをしたものでした。そうすると、必ず祖母がお団子を作って持ってきてくれました。私達は花見のお団子が一番楽しみだったのです。祖父はこれを見て、笑いながら『花より団子、花より団子』と言っていました。」

第九十課　学校　「息子の和生はぜひ国立大学に入れたいな。」「そうですね。その方が就職も楽だし、学費も私立よりずっと

226

「あ。吉本じゃないか。東京なんかで何しているんだ？」「実は息子の嫁の両親に会うために一泊二日で東京に来ているんだ。家内が君の家まであいさつに行った筈だ。」「ああ、そうかい。きたところで僕達も一緒に一杯やろうか。酒を飲ませる所を知ってていいんだ。」「ああ、そういう所が一番気楽でいいねえ。」「仕事はどうだい。うまく行っているかい。」「今のところ何とかやっているという状態だ。」「ところで君のところの息子は東京の人と結婚したんだそうだね。お金持のお嬢さんと聞いたがどうだい。」「うん。なかなかうるさい嫁で、御覧の通り東京まで両親の御機嫌をうかがいに来ているというわけだ。」「酒でも飲んで、今晩はそんな事は皆忘れよう。」「そうだ、そうだ。」

「日本のお金は、十年前に来た時と比べて随分変わりましたね」「変わらないのは、お札の紙が丈夫だという事ですね。破れたお札は見たことがありません。」「前のお札では五千円札と一万円札は同じ人物が描かれていたので、私はよく間違えました。」「それは聖徳太子という七世紀の政治家で、日本で最初の憲法を作った人です。他のお札も全部政治家で、千円札たとえば、五百円札は岩倉具視で、千円札は伊藤博文、二人とも明治時代の政治家でした。つまり、日本のお札には政治家が描かれていましたが、今度のお札には文化人が多いですね。」「一万円札は明治時代の有名な思想家の福沢諭吉です。明治維新の前に欧米旅行をしたことがあり、日本に西洋を紹介した人で、明治、大正、昭和時代の教育家

されたものです。完璧な美しさを求めていたあるお坊さんが、金閣寺のあまりの美しさに耐えられなくなって、火をつけたのだそうです。」「今の建物はコンクリートで建て直したとよく言われていますが、これは嘘です。今度も木造で建てられました。同じように完璧な美を求めていた作家の三島由紀夫がこの話を小説に書きました。題は『金閣寺』です。」「写真では建物と池の風景だけで静かな雰囲気を味わうことができますが、実際に行くと、観光客が大勢いて、金閣寺の美しさを楽しむどころではありません。」「私が行った時は、冬で、雪が降っていて、朝早かったから、まだだれもいなく、静かでした。だからそのお寺に火をつけたお坊さんの気持がわかるような気がします。」

第八十六課　上京（1.）

「ごめん下さい。」「はい、どなたですか。」「ご無沙汰しております。秋田の吉本です。」「まあ、お久し振りですね。どうぞ、お上がり下さい。」「ありがとうございます。」「そんなにご遠慮をなさらないで、どうぞお上がり下さい。けれどもお玄関で失礼いたします。ちょっと上の娘も嫁先から帰っておりますし、東京に何か御用事でいらしたのですか。」「ええ、息子の嫁の両親に会わなければならないので、一泊二日で参りました。」「よろしかったらお食事でも御一緒にいかがですか。でもまだ用事が残っていますので、こちらで失礼いたします。」「さようでございますか。せっかくお越し下さったのに……」「こちらこそ突然お訪ねして、申し訳ございません。」

宝石のついた首輪などを売っています。」
「ああ、そうですか。この間お会いした時、お宅の猫ちゃんは、すてきな宝石のついた首輪をしていましたけれど、そこで買ったんですね。」

第八十三課　文学
「この頃の若い人達はあまり本を読まなくなりましたね。私達が若かった頃には、一生懸命源氏物語や枕草子など古典文学をよく読んだものでしたが、孫などは漫画しか読みません。」「読みたい本を全部買うことはできなかったので、図書館へ通ってよく読んだものでした。二十になった頃には平安時代の主な作品はほぼ全部読んでいました。特に清少納言の枕草子などは暗記するほど何度も読みました。」「あなたは清少納言とか紫式部などの女流作家が好きなようですね。」「いいえ、別にそう言うわけではないですが、どちらかと

言うと、平安時代の朝廷文学が好きなので、自然と女の作家の作品を読むことになりました。この間、孫に『日本の代表的な古典だから源氏物語でも読みなさい』と言ったら、『もう漫画で読んだ』と答えられました。
あっ、もう四時ですね。遅くまでお邪魔しました。」「まだいいではないですか。」「え。主人が帰ってくるまでに晩御飯の買物と支度をしなければいけません。ごちそうさまでした。」「どういたしまして。又、いつでも遊びに来て下さい。」「失礼します。」「ごめん下さいませ。」

第八十五課　金閣寺
「表紙に金閣寺の写真はどうでしょうか。」「いいですね。池と金色のお寺の写真を見ると、いつも心が静まりますね。京都のお寺の中で一番きれいだと思います。今の建物は一三九七年に建てられたものではなく、一九五五年に復元

びっくりしちゃうわよ。」「片付け手伝ってくれないか。たのむよ。」

第八十一課　風邪「元気がなさそうですね。」「ええ、風邪をひきました。」「熱もあるようですね。」「ええ、今朝三十九度以上ありました。」「薬を飲むか医者に見せた方がいいですよ。」「医者も薬も嫌いです。」「私は病気になると、一切化学薬品や抗生物質を使わないで、鍼や指圧や漢方薬で直します。風邪の時は何もしないで暖かくして、寝ているだけです。」「それで直るのですか。」「はい、直ります。」「じゃあ、どうやって直すのですか。」「しかし薬を飲むよりは時間がかかります。」「僕はせっかちなので、病気が自然に直るまで待っていられません、はやく直した方がいいと思います。」

第八十二課　ペット「先週学校の生徒に見せるため、日本文化についてのビデオを何本か見ました。そこは日曜日になるとデパートの近辺の大通りが全部自動車通行禁止になり、歩行者天国になります。そして大通りの真中にテーブルや椅子を並べたり、子供のためのブランコやシーソーなども出したりします。そこまでは特に変わったことはなかったのですが、その後面白い物を見ました。日曜日に家族づれで散歩している人達の中に犬を連れている人がいましたか。その犬がどんな恰好していたと思いますか。四本の足に赤い靴をはかされていたのです。ずっと前に浅草でペット用の靴や洋服や帽子を売っている店を見たことがありますが、まさかあんな物を買う人がいるとは思いませんでした。」「このごろは動物気違いが多いのではないですか。そこでは家の近所に犬猫美容院があります。」「そこでは偽の近

第八十課　学生の部屋　「今週の金曜日」

にも左の方にも同じように人が大勢歩いて行くので、まず左へ行ってみました。改札口で切符を渡した後、エスカレーターが見えたので、上が出口かと思いました。ところが、それはデパートへ入る入口でした。やっとのおもいで、新宿駅の地下の通路へ戻って、又切符を買って、右へ行きました。今度はやっと外へ出ることができましたが、東口じゃなくて西口だったので、どこがどこだかわからなくて、タクシーでここまで来ました」。「そうですか。新宿駅は簡単ですよ。乗り換える場合には電車と同じ色の表示板がありますし、『出口』『入口』もちゃんと書いてありますから、気を付けて見れば、すぐわかるはずです」。「そうですか。でも私みたいに色盲の人はどうしたらいいんでしょう？」

におふくろが田舎から出てくるので、少し部屋を片付けなければいけないんだ」。「ど
うやってこの部屋を片付けるつもり？蒲団と机
はいつから畳んでないの。机の上にたくさんの
物が乗っているんじゃない？蒲団なんか見えない
でん部屋が一杯で、畳なんか見えないじゃ
ない？この中でどうやって勉強してるのじゃ
ないの？ワイシャツの上に野菜が置いてあって、下
着の横に砂糖が置いてある。……きたない
ナイフやフォークが机の上に置いてあっちこち
ている。時計がせっけんの下におったこっち
あるわよ。随分ひからびているせっけん随分ひからびているわよ
けど、使うことあるの」。「そりゃたまには
あるさ。僕は大学とアルバイトで夜帰っ
くると、くたくたで、部屋なんか片付ける
余裕なんてないよ」。「あなたこの前片付けた
したのはいつなの」。「この前おふくろが上京
した時だから、六ヶ月前だよ」。「それにし
ても、ちょっとひどいじゃない？お母さん

231

は大変だからやっぱりやめよう。それより
タヒチに行ってきれいな娘さん達と海岸で
踊ったり泳いだりしたいな。」「そんな夢を
見る時間があったら、書けないと言ってい
る原稿を書きなさい。お金があれば、借金
を返すことが先決でしょう。」

第七十八課　お正月の挨拶　「新年あけま
しておめでとうございます。」「あけまして
おめでとうございます。昨年中は色々とお
世話になり、ありがとうございました。」「本
年もよろしくお願いいたします。」「いや、
こちらこそ、すっかりお世話になりまして。
今年もどうぞよろしく。あ、智恵子ちゃん
は着物がよく似合って、かわいいね。」「正君も
ちゃんとお辞儀しての…」「おじさんは今年外
国へいらっしゃるのよ。」「政府の留学生と
して、ドイツへ科学の研究に二年ほど行き
ます。向こうでは学生生活をすることにな

ると思います。」「ドイツですか。私はオー
ストリアのウイーンに音楽の勉強に一年ほ
ど行ったことがあります。ドイツとオース
トリアは似ているんでしょうね。なつかし
いわ。思い出すわ。あの頃のオーストリア
での生活。あちらにいらしたら、時々手紙
を下さいね。」「なるべく書くようにします
が、最初はいそがしいから、そんなに書け
ないと思います。」「出発の日には兄とお見
送りに行きますね。」

第七十九課　新宿駅　「遅かったですね。」
「ごめんなさい。」「約束より三十分遅れて
いますよ。」「すみません。新宿駅でひどい
目にあったのです。」「どうしたんですか。」
「もう新宿駅はこりごりです。あれは駅じ
やなくて、迷路です。ホームから地下の通
路まで降りた後、どっちへ行ったらいいの
かわからなくなってしまいました。右の方

りフランスの習慣を忘れていたわ。それではシャンペンでも二人で飲みましょうか。今日は本当にご苦労様。カンパイ。」

第七十五課　キャンプ

「ここは景色がいいから、ここでテントを張ろうか。ああ、疲れたなあ……空気が澄んでいて、気持がいいな。君がテントを張っている間に、僕は晩飯の準備をしよう。この場所でテントを張ると頭が北枕になるよ。」「それじゃだめなのかい。」「日本では死人を北枕に寝かせる。だから頭を北の方向に向ける。だから日本人は北の方向に頭を向けることを嫌うんだ。」「頭が南の方に来るようにすればいいのだろう。でもそうすると、ここは斜面だから、足の方が高くなるよ。料理の方はどうだい?うまく行ってる?」「実はおしょうゆを忘れたから、味がよくないかもしれない。それにマッチが見当たらないんだ。」

「え、おしょうゆもマッチもないのか。ここまで来る途中に民宿が一つあっただろう。今夜はそこへ行った方がいいかもしれないね。」「うん。そうしよう。」

第七十六課　お金があれば

「ああ、お金があれば、こんな隙間だらけの寒い家に住まないで、セントラル・ヒーティングのある家に住みたいなあ。もしお金があれば、山中湖のそばに別荘を一軒建てて夏の二ヶ月避暑に行けば、いい原稿が書けるだろうな。」「ああ。あたしはお金があれば、ミンクのコートと鰐のハンド・バッグと大きなダイヤモンドの指輪がほしいわ。」「お金があれば皆買ってやるよ。それに、おれは光琳の絵が一枚ほしいな。世界一周もしたくないか。世界中の首都をすべて見物しようよ。」「全世界の首都に行くつもり?数年はかかるわよ。」「世界一周

お前も一杯どうだ。」「あたしはお茶の方がいいから、お湯を沸かしてきます。」「ああ、今晩は久し振りに早く寝られるな。」「そうですよ。たまには睡眠を十分取っていただかないと体がもちませんよ。」「こんばんは。自動車があったので、いらっしゃると思って…」「ああ、せっかく今晩は早く寝られると思っていたのに…」「あいつが先月行ったヨーロッパ旅行の話を始めると、夜中の一時までかかってしまうからなあ。前からおしゃべりだったのに、あの旅行に行ってからますますおしゃべりになって帰ってきたからなあ。」「さあ、ようこそいらっしゃいました。ちょうどお噂をしていたところです。…どうぞ、どうぞ…」

第七十四課　思い違い

（十二月、三十一日、五時、ミネさんは一張羅の背広を着て、藤村さんのドアのベルを鳴らす。）「あ、来てくれてちょうどよかったわ。いいの？そんなにきれいな洋服を着て…それにおみやげにシャンペンまで。ャンペンを持ってきましょう。冷蔵庫に入れて冷やしておきましょう。」（夜の八時。午後の五時から始めた大掃除がまだ終わらない。ミネさんが心配そうに）「いつお料理を作りはじめますか。」「お節料理はもうできているから、後二時間我慢すれば、家中がきれいになって、お正月を迎える準備が整うわ。」「お客さん？他のお正月の準備って大掃除のことですか。」「お客さんはいつ来るんですか。」「お客さん？今晩は、だれも来ないわよ。お掃除が終わったら、年越蕎麦を食べて、明日の朝、日の出を拝みに行って、それから年始のあいさつ回りをするのよ。」「え、今晩何もしないんですか。」「ああ、ごめんなさいね。忘れていたわ。フランスでは、大晦日に皆でレヴェイヨンをするんだったわね。すっか

ますか。」「うんうん。悪くないけれど、少し気になる事がある。」「あら、なあに?」「お見合いの写真では振り袖を着ていたからわからなかったけれど、足が太いのが気になるなあ。」「他が皆いいのだから、そのぐらいは我慢しなさい。」

第七十二課　スキー

「ウイークエンドは楽しかった?」「ひどい目にあった。もう二度とあいつとはスキーに行かない。」「あら、どうしたの。」「いつもスキーが上手だと自慢している谷沢君を知っているだろう。リフトで山の上まで行って、きれいな雪景色を見たところまではよかったのだけれど、あいつだけ降りてこないんだ。二十分近くふもとで待ったけれど、来ないから心配して、わざわざ又上まで見に行ったら、こわくて降りられないとべそをかいていた。」「それでどうしたの。」「だから子供にスキーを教えてやるように、あいつの前をゆっくりと道を作ってやりながら降りていったんだ。でも上手にカーブを曲がれないから、スピードが出て、すぐ転ぶ。その上一人で起き上がれないから、やっとのたんびに起こしてやり、半日かかって、やっと一つの山小屋から雪が降られた。その後はくたびれて山小屋から雪が降っているのを見ていただけなんだ。」「あらあら、せっかくのウイークエンドがだいなしだったわね。」

第七十三課　静かな晩

「ただいま。」「あ、お父さん。お帰りなさい。今日は早かったのね。夕食の支度がまだできてないから、お風呂にでも入って、疲れを落としていて下さい。」「うん。」「あなた、食事がでいたら、食べられますよ。」「うん、いいな。お

は皇居にごあいさつに行くことができます。宮中参賀といいます。皇居は東京の真中にあって、江戸時代の将軍のお城でした。その回りはひろびろとした公園になっていて、日曜日の朝など、そこにジョギングをしに来る人がたくさんいます。」

第六十九課　お見合い（１）

「甥の勝明は日本経済新聞の記者をしていますが、だれかいい人がないでしょうかね。」「甥御さんはおいくつですか。」「今年二十八歳で、来年の秋ブラジルに転勤することになりましたが、その前に結婚させたいのです。」「どんな方がいいのですか。」「そうですね。やっぱり大学は卒業していて、でも働いたことがなくて、向こうでは、接待が多いですから、お料理が上手で、社交性がある人が理想ですね。」「なかなかむずかしい条件ですね。」「あ、ちょっと待って下さい。そう言えば、一週間ほど前に家内が友人の国会議員のお嬢さんの写真を見せてくれました。」「あ、それはいい話ですね。」「今晩さっそく家内と話してみます。後ほど連絡いたし……（続く）

第七十一課　お見合い（２）

「とても感じのいい方ね。きれいで、はきはきしていて、社交的なところがいいわね。」「趣味も合いそうじゃない？」「勝明と同じようにスポーツや旅行、音楽が好きだと言っていたし、それに語学もよくできるそうだし、ブラジルへ行ってもきっとポルトガル語をはやく覚えるでしょう。」「向こうのお父さんもお母さんも感じがいい方達だし、彼女もお父さんが五六年前にアメリカに二年一緒に外国生活をしたから、ブラジルでも大丈夫よ。」「背もお兄さんよりちょっと小さくて、お似合いよ。」「勝明さんどう思い

第六十七課　富士山

「富士山って本当にあるのですか。」「ええ、もちろんですよ。なぜですか。」「写真や絵ではたくさん見ましたが、実物は見たことがありません。飛行機で東京へ来る時、見えることもあるそうですが、私は一遍も見たことがありません。去年の夏、伊豆半島まで出掛けました。そして山の上でこの方向に富士山があると聞きましたが、雲しか見えませんでした。知人の家族の方のお葬式で富士霊園へも行きましたが……」「あ、文学者の墓がある事で有名な、墓地ですよね。」「名前が富士霊園ですから、今度こそは富士山を見ることができるかと思いましたが、やっぱりだめでした。」「あなたが日本に来るのは夏でしょう。だから見ることができないのですよ。この次は十一月ごろいらっしゃい。そうすれば、どこからでもよく見えますよ。」「です。十一月には休みを取ることができません。だから私は一生富士山を見ることができないでしょう。」

第六十八課　皇室

「山手線の代々木駅と原宿駅の間にある駅には止まることがありませんね。」「あれは特別な駅です。」「いつも通ってもいません。今でも使っているのですか。」「もちろんです。でも特別な場合だけです。」「あれは天皇陛下がお使いになる駅なのですか。」「天皇陛下が汽車におのりになることがあるのですか。」「そうです。天皇陛下のおのりになるお乗りになります。皇居はあの駅の近くの千代田区にあります。でもそれは特別列車で、普通の人は乗ることができません。天皇陛下も夏はよく那須でいらっしゃいも皇后陛下も夏はよく那須でいらっしゃいます。」「両陛下に国民がお目にかかれる時があります。」「お正月と陛下のお誕生日にはお姿をお見せになりますので、国民

237

第六十五課　カメラを選ぶ

「新婚旅行に行く前にカメラを一つ買いたいのです。」「新宿に何軒も安いお店がありますよ。」「一緒に来てくれますか。」「いいですよ。」

一日の午後いかがですか。「はい、結構です。よろしくお願いします。」**カメラ屋で**

「小型の簡単なカメラをいくつか見せて下さい。」「そこにモデルが全部出ていますから、どうぞ手に取って御覧下さい。」「たくさんありますね。値段もついていますよ。」「あんまりあるので、どれにしたらいいかわかりません。」「全自動がいいですか。どのメーカーにしますか。予算はどのぐらいですか。今はボディーの色はいろいろありますよ。」「むずかしい選び方をしますなあ。どんな色がいいですか。」「旅行用ですから、小さくて、軽くて、僕の鞄と同じ色のこのカメラにしましょう。」「いいんですか。そんなカメラにしましょう。」

……」

第六十六課　家を建てる

石井夫妻は家を建てることについて話しあっています。

「コンクリートで建てましょう。その方が地震が来ても、安全でしょう。」「でもおれは純日本風の家の方がいいな。おれももう直定年になるから、四季を楽しめるからなあ。」「庭で盆栽でもやろうかな。」「コンクリートの家でも盆栽はできますよ。」「庭を広くするか、建物を広くするかによるな。」

「部屋数はいくつにしましょうか。まず、応接間、それに食堂も大きく取りましょう。私達の寝室と博之と江利子さんの部屋を考えて、お風呂場は日本式にして、台所はモダンにしましょう。孫達にも部屋を一つずつ準備しましょう。」「おれの庭はどうなるんだ。」「あら、もう場所がないわ。」

たのですから。この次は、急ぎの手紙には、速達で送るよりも、住所を正確に書いて下さいね。

第六十二課　銭湯

「今私が下宿しているところはお風呂もシャワーもありません。」「不便でしょう。」「ええ、でもすぐ近くに銭湯がありますから、毎晩行きます。その銭湯は立派で、湯槽は深く、ひろびろとしています。六時ごろ行くと満員ですが、夜の十時すぎはすいていて、その広い湯槽に浸かっていると、いい気持になります。それに便利な設備がいろいろあります。たとえば、お風呂に入っている間に、玄関のところに置いてある洗濯機で洗濯ができます。」「でも銭湯とは、男女別々に入るにしても、知らない人の前で裸になる所です。」「私だったら、はずかしいですね。」「でも私は全然平気です。眼鏡を取りますから、回りの人が気になりません。」

第六十四課　雑誌

「あなたの英語の勉強はいかがですか。」「ええ、大分進みました。」「どこで習っているのですか。」「個人レッスンの先生についています。やっと少し読めるようになりました。」「それじゃもう直シェークスピアでも読めるようになるでしょう。」「シェークスピアですか。僕には全然興味がありません。英語を習っているのは仕事関係の雑誌を読みたいのです。」「へえ、工業関係の仕事関係の記事を読むためですね。」「父は農業関係の仕事をしているので、その方面の雑誌も読めるようになりたいのです。」「まじめなんですね。今は全部わからなくてもどんどん読んでみることですね。あ、何か英語の雑誌を手に持っていますね。何ですか。見せて下さい。あれ、ロックの雑誌だ。」

気掃除機もね。おかしいな。これもねじが三つ足りませんよ。」「冷蔵庫もお願いできるかしら。」「奥さん、いったいどういうことですか。皆ねじが抜けています。」「主人が四ヶ月前に会社を退職しました。」それ以来、退屈して、家中の電気器具を全部分解して組み立てるのです。」「困ったことで

すね。」

第六十課　新幹線

「先週新幹線で九州の孫のところまで行きました。」「新幹線は初めてでしたか。」「はい、そうです。とても楽しかったです。六時間半しかかかりませんでした。昔と比べるとね。今の世の中は変わりました。車内から電話もかけました。しかし窓が開かないのは残念です。」「確かにそうでしょうね。それは冷房のためでしょう。外はとても蒸し暑かったのですが、新幹線の中は冷房のおかげで、涼しくて少し寒いくらいでした。椅子も座り心地がよくて眠ってしまいました。横浜から京都まで一度乗ってみたいですが、あなたも一度乗ってみたらいかがですか。」「私は毎週仕事で新幹線で大阪まで行っています。」

第六十一課　返事

手紙を確かに夕べ受け取りました。ありがとうございました。電話で速達で送ってくれたといっていたので、毎日ポストを見に行って、楽しみにしていました。ところが電話をもらってから十日後にやっと着きました。おかしいと思って、封筒をよく見たら、住所が半分しか書いてありませんでした。東京都、北区、西ヶ原まではちゃんと書いてありましたが、その後番地が抜けていました。しかも、私も有名なのですれでも着いたのですから、私も日本の郵便配達はサービスがいいのですね。わざわざ時間をかけて捜してくれ

そばを通ります。たとえば、東大寺、法隆寺、薬師寺、唐招提寺などです。小さくて静かなお寺のそばも通ります。歩いて行く車でしょう。歩いて行く人も自転車で行く人もいます。歩くと全部で十五時間ぐらいかかります。出来れば奈良に泊まって、毎日少しずつ歩いて見ることですね。」「あなたはその歴史の道を全部歩きましたか。」「以前二日だけ奈良へ行った時、三分の一歩きました。そのあと、足が痛くて、一週間近く歩くのがつらかったです。でもすばらしかったです。また行ってみたいです。」

第五十八課　選挙

「今朝、変な自動車を見ました。」「何が変だったのですか。」「えと、車の回りにたくさんの旗がついていました。それに車の上にスピーカーがついていて、盛んに何かを言っていました。」「スピーカーは何を言っていましたか。」

「人の名前を繰り返し、繰り返し、言っていました。」「ああ、それは選挙運動の自動車でしょう。大通りを走りながら、立候補者の名前を何度も繰り返して言います。」「変わった選挙運動の仕方ですね。」「日本ではそういうやりかたです。日曜日でもゆっくり休むことができません。」「選挙が近づくと町はうるさくなるでしょうね。」「そうですね。」「今回は何の選挙ですか。」「都知事選挙です。」

第五十九課　故障

「もしもし、電気屋さんですか。」こちらは竹内ですが、電気洗濯機が故障しているので、直しに来てくれますか。」「はい、かしこまりました。明日の水曜日の朝うかがいます。」次の日の朝「はい、洗濯機は直りました。」「ねじが五つ取れていました。」「あ、電気屋さん、ついでに掃除機も見てくれますか。」「はいはい、電

241

真規は帽子を忘れないで…太陽が強いから、帽子を被らないと、今晩頭が痛くなりますよ。」「わあ、水は冷たいな。あそこの岩まで競争しよう。」「いいよ。でも僕が勝つよ。」「真規は危ないから、ここでおとなしくしていなさい。」「あら、アイス・クリームを売っている。」「じゃ、この砂の上に座って食べましょう。」夜「日焼けで背中が痛くてたまらない。明日どうやって洋服を着ようかな。」

第五十五課　日本へ行く　「今年の夏のバカンスはどこへ行きますか。」「日本へ行きます。」「去年も行ったのではないですか。毎年行けて、うらやましいですね。」「ええ、そうですが、今年は汽車で行くんです。」シベリア経由の汽車で行くんです。飛行機の方が早いですが、つまらないです。でもパリからモスクワまでは飛行機で行きます。そしてモスクワで汽車に乗り換えて、ウラジオストクまで汽車で行きます。それから日本まで船か飛行機です。」「随分時間がかかるでしょう。」「ええ、しかしそれで行ったことのある友達によると、時間の感覚がなくなるので全然退屈しないそうです。」「いつ出発しますか。」「まだはっきり決めていませんが、七月の初めごろになると思います。」

第五十七課　歴史の道　「奈良に『歴史の道』というところがあるのを知っていますか。」「いいえ、聞いたことがありません。」「それは奈良の町の回りを通る道です。畑にそって、ほとんどの奈良の有名なお寺の

あの巨大な網は何ですか。」「ああ、あれ？あれはゴルフ練習場ですか。」「あれが、ゴルフ練習場です。」「日本のサラリーマンは、ゴルフをよくしますが、なかなか町の中では、練習する場所がありません。それで、広い田舎の練習場に行く代りに、上に網を張って、ゴルフ練習場を作りました。」「日本では、他にどんなスポーツをしますか。」「テニスも最近盛んになりました。」「佐々木さんは、何のスポーツが好きですか。」「野球が一番好きです。」「どこで野球をしますか。」「僕が好きなのは、テレビで見ることです。」「

第五十三課　見舞　橋本さんのお見舞に行かなければなりません。」「どこに入院しているそうですか。」「日赤病院に入院しているそうです。」「何曜日にしましょうか。」「今日は

水曜日ですから、明後日の金曜日にしましょう。**金曜日**「お見舞に何を持っていきましょうか。」「果物かお花がいいですね。」「食べ物は控えた方がいいでしょう。腸の手術だったそうですから。この赤いチューリップと黄色いチューリップを全部で十本持っていきましょう。」**病院で**「いかがですか。」「おかげさまで、大分よくなりました。あと一週間で家に帰れるそうです。」「それではお大事に。」「どうもわざわざありがとうございました。」

第五十四課　海岸で　「まず海の家を借りましょう。荷物をここに置きましょう。」「さあ、水着に着替えて、すぐ泳ぎに行きましょう。哲雄は水中眼鏡を持ちましたか。

った時だけです。お酒を飲んでいない時は現実的な人ですよ。そうでなければ、どうやって冷凍食品を売る商売ができますか。

第五十課　美術館

「ところで新しい現代美術館に行ったことがありますか。」「いいえ、まだです」「明日またはあさって一緒に見に行きましょう」「はい、ではさっそく明日の午後行きましょう。」

美術館の中で

「何を見ていますか。」「この緑色の絵を見ています。」「何ですか、これは？非常に不思議な絵ですね。私には、猫に見えます。これが足で、これが頭でしょう」「いいえ、そうではありません。猫の頭ではないと思います。」「あ、顔だと思います。」「いいえ、これは人の目で、これは鼻ですよ。猫の頭ではないと思います。」「絵の題を見ましょう。何と書いてありますか。」「夢の森」

第五十一課　タクシー

「レストラン・ナポレオンまで急いでおねがいします。」「え、何ですか。」「ナポレオンという名前のフランス料理のレストランです。」「あ、港区にあるのですか、と聞きました。」「サントリー美術館のすぐそばにある美術館ですね。」

美術館の前

「ここがサントリー美術館です。これからどう行きますか。」「これが住所です。」「住所だけではわからないな。」「あそこのにぎやかな所に公衆電話があると思いますから、電話でくわしい道を聞いてみます。」「こまかいお金を持っていますか。」「十円玉をたくさん持っているから、大丈夫です。」

電話をかけてから

「友達が迎えに来ますから、ここで降りることにします。」

第五十二課　スポーツ

「電車から見える

い胃を休ませるために、少し食物を控えて下さい。」「でも今晩、昇進祝いにフランス・レストランに行くことになっていますが……」

第四十七課　音楽

カクテル・パーティーで。「何かお飲みになりますか。シャンペンはお好きですか。加藤さんから音楽がお好きだとうかがいましたが……」「はい。特にクラシック音楽が好きです。」「何か楽器をなさっていますか。」「オーボエをやっているのですか。」「五、うどのぐらいなさっているのですか。」「六年です。」「高等学校の時クラブ活動で始めたのがきっかけです。卒業してからなかなか吹く機会がありません。ですから最近は自分で吹くより、もっぱらレコードやカセットやラジオを聞いています。」「僕の家にいる時はラジオをつけっぱなしです。」「家にいる時

音楽好きの仲間が十二人ぐらい日曜日に隔週で集まります。よろしかったら、いらっしゃいませんか。」「ぜひ仲間に入れて下さい。」その方が一人で練習するより楽しいです。

第四十八課　秋の日の……

「もうそろそろ夏が終わりますね。　秋の足音が聞こえるみたいですね。いわし雲が浮かんでいる空や夕焼けを見ると、この世が空しくなります。枯葉が落ちるのを見ていると悲しくなります。全く『秋の日のビオロンの溜息……』の詩のようですな。　夏の終わりの日暮れの太陽の光が庭の柿の木の葉に輝いているのを見ると、もう秋になってしまったのかと思います。時があまりにも早く過ぎるので、寂しい気持になります。」「あら、人の命なんてはかないものですよ。　あなたのご主人はロマンチックな方ですね。

245

第四十五語　銀行「度々日本に来るから、口座を開きたいのですが……口座は簡単に開くことができますか。」「はい。口座は簡単に開くことができます。普通口座なら、外国人でも開くことができます。」「それでは、私も口座を開きましょう。後二日でカナダへ帰ります。帰国の前に、残った日本円を預けていくことにします」「普通口座でも利子がつきますから、来年の冬また日本に遊びに来る時、お金が増えています。じゃ、明日一時半に銀行の前で会いましょう。」　翌日、銀行の前で「予定外の買物をしたので、お財布が空っぽになってしまいました。だから口座を開くことができなくなりました。それに空港までのバス代もなくなってしまいました。空港では飛行場使用料も払わなければなりません。こんなお願いで悪いけれど、一万円貸してくれませんか。」

第四十六課　医者「あなたが胃が痛いと言っていましたので、私が知っているお医者さまに予約を取りました。」「ありがとうございます。」「胃潰瘍ではないかと心配しています。」「それは早くお医者さんへ行ったほうがいいですね。このごろは胃潰瘍でも早く治療すると、問題なく直るそうですから」「それで予約はいつですか。」「再来週の水曜日の午後四時十五分前です。」病院「おかけ下さい。どうなさいましたか。」「食後一時間ぐらい経つと、胃がじんと痛くなります。胃潰瘍ではないでしょうか。」「ちょっと見てみましょう。舌を出して下さい。そのベッドに横になって下さい。ここを押すと、痛いですか。」「いいえ。」「ここは？」「いいえ。」「ここは？」「いいえ。」「大丈夫です。わかりました。何でもありません。ただの食べすぎです。一週間ぐら

大丈夫だと言うのです。マノリータはいつもこの調子ですが、とても温かい人なので、友達がたくさんいます。今度紹介します。」

第四十三課　Ｓ.Ｆ.

「あさって映画を見に行きます。」「どんな映画を見るのですか。」「僕はＳ.Ｆ.が大好きです。あさって見に行こうと思っている映画は『宇宙冒険』といいます。」「僕はもう見ました。おもしろいですよ。」それは二千五百六年に起こる物語です。地球のロケットの出発点は月です。そして他の星と惑星の果てへそこから地球を飛び立つのです。でも宇宙の果てから地球を侵略する悪者が出てきます。ヒーローは地球の安全を守るために、宇宙の彼方まで冒険に行くのです。そして敵国の悪者の妹に恋をするのです。最後はハッピ・エンドです。」「それなら宇宙冒険ですね。話の内容を全部聞いてしまったのでもう見に行く気がしません。僕には、恋の冒険なんて興味がありません。」

第四十四課　ホテル

「おはようございます。プリンス・ホテルでございます。」「部屋の予約をおねがいしたいのですけれども……」「お一人さまですか。」「いいえ、家内と子供が二人います。」「大人二人、子供二人全部で四名さまですね。ご滞在はいつまででですか。」「来月の十二日から十五日までおねがいしたいのですが…」「来月は大変混んでおりますので、ちょっと離れた二部屋ですが、よろしいでしょうか。」「同じ階ですか。」「はい、そうでございます。」「よろしくおねがいします。」「チェック・インの時間は正午からでございます。」「（妻に）部屋の予約をしたよ。ちょっと離れている部屋だけど同じフロアだって。」「それじゃ、仕方がないわね。まあ、いいわ。」

並んでいたので見ることができませんでした。その代わり、お祖父さんがパンダの絵葉書を一枚ずつ買ってくれました。とても楽しい一日でした。

第四十課　工場見学

「ようこそいらっしゃいました。これから私共の工場をご案内しましょう。ここでは電気製品を主に作っています。どうぞ、こちらへ。足元に気をつけて下さい。ここはできあがった電気製品の倉庫です。できた年代ごとに置いてあります。右の建物は事務所です。左の建物は製造工場です。」「すみませんが、ちょっと質問があるのですけれども…」「どうぞ。何ですか。」「工員が全然見えませんが、どこにいるのですか。」「前は工員がしていた仕事を今はロボットが全部しています。」「前はロボットを動かしていたコンピュータがロボットを動かしていますよ。」「失業者は出なかったのですか。」「工員は私達が持っているロボットを作る工場とコンピュータを組立てる工場で働いています。」

第四十一課　変わった人

「私の友達のマノリータに会ったことがありますか。」「会ったことがありません。」「とてもおもしろいアルゼンチン人です。」「職業は？」「作曲家です。」「女の作曲家ですか。めずらしいですね。」「そうですね。でもマノリータは変わった人です。今オペラを作曲しているそうです。とてもいそがしいと言っていますが、他の約束は断るのに、マージャンに誘うと必ず来ます。この間も、アルゼンチン料理をごちそうしてくれるといったので、楽しみにしていました。前の日から病気だったそうです。三時間前に電話がかかってきました。そうです。ですから食後にするマージャンは

248

第三十八課　書類

「この書類はわからないところがたくさんありますから、説明して下さい。」「名前と苗字の意味はわかりますが、国籍とは何ですか。」「国籍というのはあなたはどこの国の人ですかということです。必ずしも生まれた国ではありません。たとえば由美さんはオーストラリアで生まれましたが、国籍は『スペイン』です。」「住所はわかりますが、あなたの国籍は『日本』ですね。」「職業とはどういう意味ですか。」「あなたがしている仕事のことです。この書類は何のための物ですか。大学に入学するためですか。滞在許可証のためですか。」「いいえ。テニス・クラブに入るためです。」

第三十九課　両親への手紙

おとといの木曜日はお祖父さんとお祖母さんと上野の動物園へ行ってきました。私達は初めて動物園へ行ったので、大喜びでした。一時間以上並びました。「どうしてこんなに皆並ぶのですか」とお祖父さんに聞きました。「春は子供が生まれる季節なので、皆見にくるのです」とお祖父さんが答えました。先ず首が長いきりんを見ました。それからしわだらけの三頭の象を見ました。一頭は耳が小さいアフリカ象でした。もう二頭は耳が大きいインド象でした。愛嬌がいい熊はピーナッツをむしゃむしゃ食べていました。川崎先生によく似た猿が木の枝から枝へ移っていました。眠そうな目をしたらくだがゆっくり歩いていました。ライオンが檻の中で吠えた時には、妹のかおるちゃんが驚いて泣きました。きっとこわかったのでしょう。パンダの檻の前はたくさんの人が

249

第三十六課　苗字

「日本人の苗字は自然の物を表す名前が多いですね。」「そうですね。それに同じ苗字を持っている人がたくさんいます。電話帳には同じ苗字が何ページも続くことがあります。たとえば、山田とか田中とか鈴木などという名前です。」「どうしてそんなに同じ名前の人がいるのですか。皆親戚の人ですか。」「いいえ。必ずしもそういうわけではありません。昔は公家と武家の人しか苗字がありませんでした。段々平民も苗字を持つことになりました。平民は田舎に住んでいる人がほとんどでした。どういう苗字をつけようかと思った時、自然に関係がある苗字を作りました。たとえば、山に田を持っていた人は『山田』という苗字になりました。『渡辺』という名前は川を渡る所に住んでいた人につけた名前です。『山中』という名前は山の中に

第三十七課　ハチ公(続き)

「ハチ公は秋田犬ですから、飼い主によく仕えます。でもそのうちに上野さんは亡くなりました。それでもハチ公は毎日上野さんを迎えに行きました。毎日何時間も待ちましたが、上野さんは帰ってきませんでした。何年間もの間、ハチ公は毎日上野さんを迎えに行きました。ある日、ハチ公も死にました。渋谷の人々はハチ公に感心したので、駅の前にハチ公の銅像を建てることにしました。今日本中の人々はハチ公の銅像は有名です。渋谷駅の前ではハチ公の銅像が皆その話を知っています。人と会う約束をする時、人々は必ず『ハチ公の銅像の前で会いましょう』と言いま

がかかります。急いでいる時は汽車か飛行機で旅行した方が早いです。それに高速道路はいつも有料ですから高くつきます。」「関西はいかがでしたか。」「それが…静岡辺りでスピード違反でパトカーに捉まってしまいました。すごい罰金を払うことになりました。それで予算が足りなくなったので、そのまま東京に戻りました。」

第三十三課　ハチ公　「渋谷駅の前にある犬の銅像は何ですか。」「これはハチ公という犬の銅像です。」「なぜ犬の銅像などを作ったのですか。」「これは話すと長くなりますが……ハチ公という犬はとても感心な犬でした。六十年前のことです。上野英三郎さんという大学の先生がいました。ハチ公という犬を飼っていました。毎朝上野さんが大学へ行く時、ハチ公はいつも駅までおくって行きました。夕方上野さんが大学から帰ってくる時、ハチ公はかならず迎えに行きました。」「かわいい犬ですね。」（続く）

第三十四課　不動産屋さん　「青山辺りに家を捜しているのですが、何かありませんか。」「アパートですか、一軒家ですか。」「庭つきの一軒家に住みたいです。庭は大きい方がいいです。妻がお茶と生け花をしますから、八畳ぐらいの和室もほしいです。車が二台入るガレージも必要ですし、台所はどうしますか。」「お客が多いので、便利に使える台所がいいです。家賃はどのぐらいになりますか。」「一ヶ月百万円です。それに敷金と礼金は二ヶ月分です。だから入居する時全部で五百万円になります。」「そんなに高いのですか。私には払うことができません。あきらめます。」

岸にだれもいません。朝日が水平線から出てくる眺めはすばらしいです。日中はとても暑いです。村の人は働いていますが私は昼寝をしていました。島で食べた魚や貝類はとてもおいしかったです。その日に釣れた魚ですから、とても新鮮です。また来年の夏も行くつもりです。」「うらやましいですね。」

第三十一課　バーゲン

「旅行に出る前に、小さい手提鞄とタオルを三枚と香水が買いたいです。」「今三越デパートがバーゲンをしていますから、そこで買いましょう。散歩がてら東京駅から歩いて行きましょう」「それはいい考えですね。」「あ、雨が降ってきましたから、地下鉄に乗りましょう。」「あそこにかかっている赤いタオルはどんな色がいいですか。」「ペアで買いましょう。」「それと三枚目のタオルにはその横にある白いタオルはいかが。」「あ、この傘は安いですね。主人がこの間姉からもらった傘を電車に忘れたのですよ。あら、この水色の縁がついたガウンも安いですね。」**一時間後**「さあ帰りましょう。帰りに銀行に寄ってもいいですか。お金を全部使ってしまいましたので……」

第三十二課　高速道路

「伯父が自動車を貸してくれたので、先週の週末、会社の同僚と関西旅行をするつもりで出発しました。」「いかがでしたか。」「最初は国道を走りましたが、混んでいましたので、高速道路で行くことにしました。高速道路ではスピード制限が八十キロなので、早く進みませんでした。それにトラックがたくさん走っていました。トラックを追い越すことはむずかしいです。ですから日本での自動車旅行は時間

きます。」「飛行場まで迎えに行きますから
ね。」「朝早いから、箱崎のエア・ターミナ
ルまでリムジン・バスで行きます。そこで
会いましょう。」「大丈夫ですよ。早く会い
たいから飛行場まで行きます。必ず行きま
すから、待っていて下さい。」「荷物はたくさんあります
悪いわね。」「荷物はたくさんありますか。」
「小さいバッグ二つだけです。」「そうですか。」
れだけ。おみやげは?」「心配しないで。い
い物を買って来ました。」「じゃ。兄と一緒
に税関を出た所で待っています。」「それで
は、よろしくおねがいします。」

第二十九課　誕生日

「今度の火曜日は、
あなたの誕生日だから、どこかでお食事し
ましょう。それからお芝居か音楽会に行か
ない?」「てんぷらが食べたいな。」「じゃそ
れなら上原さんが教えてくれたお店に行き
ましょう。」「ぴあはどこ。」「そこのピアノ

の上にあるから取って。お芝居は何ページ
に出ている?音楽会は?音楽会なら今サモ
ロビッチが日本に来ているから、聞きに行
きましょう。それとも歌舞伎なら今五三郎
が『四谷怪談』をやっているわよ。あなた
はサモロビッチと五三郎とどっちがいいの。
あ、ちょっと待って。火曜日はサモロビッ
チの演奏はないわ。歌舞伎にしましょう。
あたしが切符を買っておくわ。」「じゃたの
むよ。」「あ、これ先週のぴあよ。」

第三十課　夏休み

「お久しぶりですね。
きれいに小麦色に焼けましたね。夏休みは
どこへ行ったのですか。」「大島へ行ってき
ました。瀬戸内海の西にある島です。そこ
の名物はみかんです。そこは太陽の光が強
いです。ですから、一日中泳ぐか昼寝しか
できません。毎朝六時半に起きました。そ
して海へ泳ぎに行きました。その時間は海

第二十五課　小説

「今小説を書いています。」「へえ、どんな小説ですか」「推理小説です。」「出版するつもりですか。」「まだわかりません。」「どんな話ですか。」「主人公はファッション・モデルです。知らないでスパイと結婚します。」「おもしろそうですね。何ページぐらいになりますか。」「五百ページぐらいになると思います。」

「ートがみつかりました。とても狭いです。」「それは便利ですね。駅から歩いて五分です。」「でもうるさくありませんか。」「電車の音は全然聞こえませんが、隣の幼稚園の子供がうるさいです。」「何階ですか。」「四階です。」「眺めはいかがですか」「それが…ちょうど向かいに二十階のビルが立っていますから、何も見えません。家賃だけが気に入っています。」それほど高くありません。」

第二十六課　中国へ行く

「来年の春に中国へ行くつもりでした。」「中国語はできますか。」「私はできません。けれども息子はよくできますから、つれて行くつもりでした。しかし息子は都合が悪くなりました。」「中国へ何をしに行きますか。」「仕事と観光です。」「私は中国語が少しできますから、お供しましょうか。」「それはたすかります。今度の月曜日の晩一緒に食事をしましょう。」「はい、そうしましょう。」

第二十七課　飛行場に着く

「もしもし。正子です。」「飛行機は決まりましたか。いつ着きますか。」「日航の四百五十三便で、しあさっての午前七時十五分に成田空港に着

第二十課　禁煙

「この辺にタバコ屋がありますか。」「あります。」「遠いですか。」「いいえ、そんなに遠くありません。」「どこですか。」「本屋の隣です。それから左にまがります。右側に大きい本屋があります。その隣です。」「ありがとうございます。たすかりました。三日前から禁煙していましたが、続きませんでした。」「つらいですね。僕も禁煙していますが、タバコがすいたいな。」「それでは一緒にタバコ屋へ行きましょう。」

第二十二課　郵便局

「郵便局はどこにありますか。」「すぐ後ろにあります。」「あ。これは、どうもありがとう。ギリシャへの航空郵便葉書の料金はいくらですか。」「イギリスまでですか。」「いいえ。ギリシャまでです。」「ギリシャまでではありません。ギリシャまでです。」

「ああ。ギリシャですか。ちょっとお待ち下さい。今調べますから。はい、ありました。ギリシャまでは、葉書一枚、百十円です。十枚で千百円になります。」「はい。千百円です。」「ありがとうございます。」

第二十三課　仕事

「上の息子さんはお元気ですか。」「今年大学を卒業しました。」「東大でしたね。」「はい、そうです。」「それはおめでとうございます。どこにお勤めですか。」「四月から自動車関係の会社に勤めています。」「それはよろしいですね。」「でも今入院しています。五月に交通事故にあいました。」「それはお気の毒に。その後いかがですか。」「おかげさまで、よくなりました。来週退院します。」「安心しまし

第二十四課　アパート

「やっといいアパ

え、その左の茶碗です。」「ええと・・・これは
三万円です。」「三万円ですか。高いです
ね。」「あ、ごめんなさい。三千円です。」
「ちょっと見せて下さい。」「はい、どう
ぞ。」「古いものですか。」「そうですよ。江
戸時代のものです。」「ではこれを下さい。」
はい三千円。」「どうもありがとうございま
す。」「あれ。茶碗の裏に『Made In Hong
Kong』と書いてある。やられた。」

第十八課　本屋「いらっしゃいませ。」
「トルストイの『戦争と平和』はあります
か。」『戦争と平和』ですか。はい、ありま
す。しょうしょうお待ち下さい。」「それから
料理の本を見せて下さい。」「日本料理です
か、フランス料理ですか、中華料理です
か。」「実は今家内が留守です。自分で料理
をしなければなりません。」「それではこの
本をおすすめします。実は私もこれで作り

ます。簡単にできます。」「それではこれに
します。」「毎度ありがとうございます。」

第十九課　コンサート「このうつくし
い人はだれですか。」「この写真の人です
か。」「はい、そうです。」「山口文子です。」
「女優ですか。」「いいえ、女優ではありま
せん。歌手です。」「どんな歌を歌います
か。」「ジャズです。こんどの土曜日にサ
ン・プラザでコンサートがあります。一緒
にいかがですか。」「とてもざんねんです
が、都合がわるいです。」「ざんねんですね。写
真よりもっとうつくしい人ですよ。」「ほん
とう？約束をやめようかな。でもそれはむ
りだなあ。」「それではまたこの次の機会に
お誘いしましょう。」「ぜひおねがいしま
す。」

256

う。」「いらっしゃいませ。」「山田さんは何にしますか。」「私はコーヒー。」「じゃあ、コーヒーとビールを下さい。お菓子を食べましょうか。」「いいえ、けっこうです。」「本当ですか。」「ええ、本当にけっこうです。」「ああ、そうですか。今ダイエットをしていますか。」「ええ、しています。」「いつから。」「昨日から。」

第十三課　約束　「今朝フランス人の友達をデパートの前で一時間待ちましたね。」「随分待ちましたね。」「はい。」「来ましたか。」「いいえ、来ませんでした。」「どうしたのでしょう。」「わかりません。」「こまりましたね。」「ええ、買物ができませんでした。今晩友達に電話をします。」

第十五課　紹介　「小林道子と申します。三年前に結婚しました。東京に住んでいます。子供が二人います。女の子と男の子です。」「お嬢さんはいくつですか。」「今十五歳です。」「え?」「お坊ちゃんはいくつですか。」「まだ一歳です。」「実は三年前に再婚しましたか。」

第十六課　日曜日　「今日は日曜日です。お天気がいいですね。ピクニックに行きましょうか。」「いいですね。田中さんと山本さんを誘いましょう。」「どこへ行きましょうか。」「ああそれはいい考えですね。」「江ノ島はいかがですか。何を持って行きましょうか。」「サンド・ウイッチにお寿司にみかんにお菓子。子供のためにジュースも持って行きましょう。」「田中さんと山本さんにすぐ電話をかけましょう。」「はい。おねがいします。」

第十七課　のみの市　「その箱の右の茶碗はいくらですか。」「これですか。」「いい

くさんあります。」

第八課　映画　「昨日何をしましたか。」「友達が来ました。一緒に映画に行きました。」「何の映画を見ましたか。」「アメリカの映画を見ました。チャップリンの『モダン・タイムズ』を見ました。」「おもしろかったですか。」「わかりません。眼鏡を忘れました。よく見えませんでした。」

第九課　中華料理　「今晩中華料理を食べましょうか。」「ああ、いいですね。中華料理が大好きです。」「私も。スープと肉と魚をとりましょう。」「そうですね。」「お箸で食べますか。」「いいえ、フォークで食べます。」「おねがいします。フォークを下さい。」「はい、どうぞ。」「ありがとう。おいしいですか。」「とてもおいしいです。」「また来ましょう。」

第十課　テレビ　「お相撲を見ましたか。」「はい、テレビで見ました。」「またお相撲のシーズンですね。」「そうですね。」「またお相撲のテレビを見ますか。」「時々見ます。」「よくテレビで何を見ますか。」「ニュースとホーム・ドラマを見ます。」「どちらが好きですか。」「どちらも好きです。」

第十一課　朝　「朝何時に起きますか。」「十一時に起きます。」「遅いですね。夜何時に寝ますか。」「夜中の三時に寝ます。」「でも今日は十時に起きました。」「それでも遅いですね。」「午後から夜中までバーで働いています。」「それならわかります。大変ですね。」

第十二課　喫茶店　「こんにちは。」「あそこの喫茶店へ行きましょ

第一課　「早く。行きましょう。」「どこへ。」「あそこへ。」「わかりました。どこへ。」「あそこへ。」「暑いですね。」「そうですね。」

第二課　ピカソ展　「見ましたか。」「何を。」「ピカソ展。」「まだです。」「いいですよ。」「そうですか。あした行きます。」

第三課　朝食　「おはようございます。」「おはようございます。」「パンを食べますか。」「食べます。」「コーヒーを飲みますか。」「飲みます。」「ビールを飲みますか。」「飲みません。」「りんごを食べますか。」「食べません。」「それでは卵を食べますか。」「食べます。」

第四課　税関　「カメラを持っていますか。」「はい、持っています。」「どこにあります　か。」「トランクの中にあります。」「トラン

クの中に何がありますか。」「洋服と本があります。」「それだけですか。」「はい、そうです。」「お酒？」「ありません。」「はい、けっこうです」

第五課　買物　「どこへ行きますか。」「デパートへ行きます。」「一緒に行きます。何を買いますか。」「靴下を買います。」「着きました。入りましょう。」「ここに靴下があります。」「でも高いですね。」「そうですね。やめます。」

第六課　東京タワー　「東京タワーを知っていますか。」「はい、知っています。」「ここからどう行きますか。」「まず目黒駅まで歩きます。近いです。そこから渋谷駅まで電車で行きます。それから渋谷駅からタワーまでバスで行きます。タワーに水族館があります。おもしろいです。おみやげの店もた

INDEX

This index here is presented in the same way as indices of Japanese books. The kanji are listed:

1. By number of strokes: it is therefore important to know how many strokes are in the character you are looking for! That's why we have given you the necessary numbers at the introduction of each kanji.

2. When more than one kanji have the same number of strokes—as is often the case—then they are classified according to the order of their radical (take another look at Appendix 1). When two kanji have the same radical and the same stroke order, they are put in order by pronunciation.

Across from each kanji is the page number where you will find it in this volume.

地	83	住	43	決	70	周	173
多	97	体	167	沢	165	味	101
好	35	伯	87	状	188	命	129
字	98	伴	206	男	45	和	51
存	203	余	178	町	133	国	68
安	63	冷	130	社	62	夜	37
宇	114	初	88	私	35	奈	139
守	52	別	96	究	174	妻	96
宅	181	利	64	系	202	始	125
寺	140	努	198	臣	201	姉	85
当	40	労	169	良	139	姓	204
州	204	医	120	花	96	妹	109
年	44	卵	23	見	22	学	60
式	157	君	165	言	20	季	106
成	71	告	197	谷	29	官	201
早	19	吹	125	豆	159	実	45
曲	113	吠	109	貝	81	宙	114
有	91	呂	150	赤	84	定	119
机	177	囲	186	走	89	宝	181
次	55	困	200	足	93	居	74
死	102	図	182	身	195	屈	138
毎	53	坊	46	車	29	岸	80
気	46	売	130	近	29	岩	136
江	47	完	184	迎	71	岡	91
池	184	寿	47	返	142	店	30
百	59	局	58	里	206	府	174
竹	143	廷	183	阪	148	彼	116
米	191	弟	204	麦	77	念	147
考	47	形	205			怪	75
耳	107	応	156	**8 strokes**		性	163
肉	35	忘	33	事	59	所	73
自	52	我	165	京	27	房	147
舌	122	戻	93	供	44	押	122
色	78	抗	179	使	86	招	141
芝	74	抄	202	舎	100	拝	168
行	20	抜	145	具	145	放	195
西	79	改	175	典	182	政	174
		条	163	並	106	昇	123
7 strokes		束	40	制	89	昔	100
		村	81	卒	60	明	73
何	22	来	32	参	162	服	25
作	52	求	185	取	75	果	115
似	108	汽	90	受	148	枝	108

263

枕	170	係	61	洗	144	食	23
東	27	侵	116	浅	180	首	106
杯	102	信	193	派	150	香	82
板	176	便	58	洋	24		
枚	59	侶	207	点	115	**10 strokes**	
林	43	前	41	狭	64	個	153
欧	191	則	206	界	173	候	143
武	100	南	170	畑	140	借	135
步	28	品	111	発	88	修	205
毒	63	型	154	皆	99	倉	111
泳	80	城	162	皇	160	値	154
泣	109	変	38	盆	156	俳	205
治	121	奏	76	相	36	凍	130
注	203	姿	161	研	174	帰	85
波	194	客	97	砂	137	勉	152
泊	141	室	96	祝	123	原	74
沸	167	封	149	祖	105	員	112
法	140	屋	50	科	174	哲	135
版	67	単	53	秋	102	唐	141
物	26	度	53	紀	186	夏	77
画	31	建	102	約	40	娯	196
的	129	後	38	美	103	娘	157
直	122	待	41	耐	185	孫	146
盲	176	急	90	胃	120	家	51
知	28	思	68	背	137	宮	161
空	58	恰	180	草	180	容	117
突	187	指	172	荘	171	将	162
者	112	持	24	茶	39	展	21
育	192	故	62	茹	198	島	47
英	94	映	31	要	97	師	141
苦	169	昨	31	軍	162	席	202
若	181	春	68	送	149	庫	111
苗	98	昭	191	退	63	座	117
表	98	是	145	追	90	庭	95
邪	178	星	115	迷	175	徒	180
金	58	昼	80	郎	75	息	60
長	68	冒	114	重	199	恋	116
雨	83	枯	127	限	89	挙	142
青	84	柿	128	面	153	振	164
非	131	染	198	音	64	搜	95
		段	100	風	129	捉	92
9 strokes		海	78	飛	70	捕	204
乗	84	活	125			料	34

旅	82	除	144	球	115	鳥	198		
晦	168	陛	161	現	129	黄	135		
時	37	高	27	理	34	黒	28		
書	50			産	95				
案	110	**11 strokes**		略	116	**12 strokes**			
桜	192	偽	180	盛	134	傘	85		
校	124	側	57	眼	33	備	151		
栽	156	動	61	眺	66	割	203		
残	118	務	111	移	108	勤	61		
殊	197	商	130	窓	146	勝	137		
浸	151	問	112	第	19	喜	105		
浜	148	堂	157	符	76	喫	38		
浮	126	婚	44	経	122	善	193		
流	183	寄	86	終	126	場	70		
特	124	寂	128	紹	42	報	199		
留	52	宿	150	組	113	奥	145		
疲	166	崎	71	習	20	寒	148		
病	113	常	131	翌	119	富	158		
真	53	帳	98	船	138	就	194		
眠	109	強	79	菓	39	帽	136		
破	189	張	134	菜	177	弾	203		
笑	194	得	206	術	130	複	184		
紙	105	御	154	規	136	悲	127		
純	155	悪	69	視	190	惑	115		
納	183	戚	99	許	104	換	138		
航	58	掛	159	設	151	提	82		
荷	72	控	123	訪	188	散	83		
華	33	授	195	訳	188	景	166		
袖	165	推	67	貨	189	暑	20		
被	136	接	156	転	141	晴	199		
記	153	掃	144	週	63	晩	34		
財	119	描	189	進	89	普	118		
起	37	教	74	都	55	最	88		
軒	95	斜	170	部	86	替	135		
造	186	断	113	郵	57	朝	22		
速	86	族	30	酔	129	椅	148		
通	62	械	160	野	94	森	132		
途	171	混	89	釣	81	温	114		
連	164	済	163	険	114	湖	171		
酒	25	渋	29	隆	140	港	71		
配	72	深	151	雪	166	渡	101		
院	62	清	182	頃	175	湯	150		
降	83	涼	147	魚	36	満	151		

静	91	縁	85	糖	177	観	69
鞄	82	線	80	縫	196	顔	131
駅	28	舞	75	興	117	題	122
鳴	168	蔵	144	薬	140	類	81
鼻	132	蕎	168	親	99		

15 strokes

		課	19	諺	192	**19 strokes**	
億	164	誕	73	論	190	瀬	78
儀	173	談	76	頼	195	繰	142
劇	196	調	59	避	172	羅	167
器	124	質	112	隣	57	警	200
嘘	185	賓	200	頭	107	鏡	33
噂	167	趣	124	館	30	離	117
嬌	107	輝	128			願	120
幣	189	輩	192	**17 strokes**			
慮	187	輪	172	優	54	**20 strokes**	
撲	36	選	142	濯	144	懸	181
敵	116	震	155	療	121	競	137
敷	97	霊	159	覧	154	籍	103
横	84			講	197	議	131
槽	150	**16 strokes**		鍼	179	鰐	172
潰	121	嬢	45	鮮	82		
澄	169	憲	190			**21 strokes**	
熱	178	整	168	**18 strokes**		魔	184
確	147	曇	199	曜	46		
稿	172	機	55	壁	185	**22 strokes**	
箱	48	橋	134	簡	52	驚	109
箸	36	燃	185	職	103		
		築	205	藤	123		

BIBLIOGRAPHY

Kanji Manuals

Wolfgang HADAMITSKY, Mark SPAHN. *Kanji and Kana*. Rutland (Vermont), Tokyo: Tuttle, 1981.

P. G. O'NEILL. *Essential Kanji*: 2,000 Basic Japanese Characters Systematically Arranged For Learning And Reference. New York: Weatherhill, 1987.

Reiko SUZUKI, Are HAJIKANO, Sayuri KATAOKA. *Business Kanji*. Rutland (Vermont), Tokyo: Tuttle, 1999.

Kanji Dictionaries

The New Nelson Japanese-English Character Dictionary / based on the classical Edition by Andrew N. NELSON, completed, revised by John H. HAIG. Rutland (Vermont), Tokyo: Tuttle, 1999.

Kodansha's Essential Kanji Dictionary. Tokyo: Kodansha International, 2002.

The Kodansha Kanji Learner's Dictionary / by Jack HALPHERN. Tokyo: Kodansha International, 1999.

Aubin Imprimeur
LIGUGÉ, POITIERS

Achevé d'imprimer en février 2007
N° d'édition 2534 / N° d'impression P 70710
Dépôt légal, février 2007
Imprimé en France

Reliure : BRUN à Malesherbes